Dear Ones,
As you pursue truth, I pray you discover love.
In a world gone harsh, you must have the courage to
be tender as a blossom and tough as a diamond.
Stand faithful. Stand true. Stand strong.
In word and deed light the way to the rock of refuge.
Be confident. You cannot fail for you were
hewn from the invincible stone.

"There's no foundation more solid than the Rock on which we're called to build our lives, our marriages, and our dreams. Lisa's new book, *Adamant*, will challenge you to discover more about who God is, and in turn, more about who you are."

Steven Furtick, pastor, Elevation Church;
New York Times bestselling author

"There is so much uncertainty in our world today. It's hard to know what or who to believe. That's why Lisa Bevere's new book, *Adamant*, is powerfully relevant. Lisa writes with confidence, poise, and grace as she leads you on a spiritual journey toward unshakable truth. Her words are timeless and timely, inviting us back to a place of sanctity, stability, and truth grounded in Christ."

Craig and Amy Groeschel, pastors of Life.Church;
authors of *From This Day Forward*

"Important. Weighty. Convicting. Lisa Bevere is relentless in her conviction to stand on and for the Truth. Her clarion voice reminds us that Truth has a Name, and it's a Name we can know. If you're longing for an unshakable place to anchor your life (and all of us are), *Adamant* will help lead you to the only unchanging Rock—Jesus. Keep this book nearby, and more often, keep its conviction-filled pages open in your hands."

Louie and Shelley Giglio, founders of Passion Conferences

"Wow! My dear friend Lisa hit a home run: 'When truth becomes fluid, we lose contact with answers larger than ourselves. Real truth is a Rock. Adamant. Indivisible. Immovable. Invincible.' In a generation and culture where truth moves with the trends, the scriptural truths Lisa shares in this book are so greatly needed."

Christine Caine, bestselling author and founder
of The A21 Campaign and Propel Women

"Like a beautiful tapestry made of the most elegant fabric, *Adamant* combines Lisa Bevere's undeniable passion, vulnerability, and divine gift as wind to set each reader free. With love and understanding, Bevere takes us on a journey that will transform your mind, heal your heart, and fill your spirit with the revelation of God's perfect plan for your life."

Sarah Jakes Roberts, author of *Don't Settle for Safe*

"This book is profound in its wisdom, yet deeply personal. Lisa is a gifted writer and a trusted friend who will guide us to a rock-solid understanding of our true identity in Christ."

Sheila Walsh, author of *In the Middle of the Mess*

"In reading the opening pages of this bold new work, two statements resonate with my experience of the Christ and his Kingdom. 'When stripped of awe, we find ourselves clothed in confusion and comparison' and 'when truth becomes fluid, we lose contact with answers that are bigger than ourselves.' These two realities are as profound as it gets when it comes to the human condition. I am excited for what this book will stir, affirm, and ignite. In a world grasping for genuine reality, may you find wisdom for the journey, confidence of conviction, grace to be the child you truly are, and boldness to become light in the darkness for others."

Bobbie Houston, co-senior pastor of Hillsong Church

"Lots of preachers and authors talk about living an 'Adamant' life for Jesus, but Lisa Bevere truly defines it. This book is Holy Spirit–breathed, and the anointing on her life through this book is evident."

Heather Lindsey, author/speaker

"I'll never forget the moment Lisa shared with me her plans to write her new book, *Adamant*. Sitting in my car, tears streaming down my face, I was struck with this very moving and relevant topic. In a world that sees truth as relative, Lisa masterfully tackles difficult topics, answers unearthing questions, and builds a biblical foundation we can lean on for years to come. Lisa has done it again! She writes the books we all love to read but also find ourselves needing to read at the same time."

Havilah Cunnington, co-founder of Truth to Table

"I'm so excited for this new book from Lisa! She is such a dear friend of ours, and she carries such a timely word for this hour. She and John have been incredible friends and leaders in our lives, and we absolutely love what God is doing in and through them."

Brian and Jenn Johnson, founders of Bethel Music

ADAMANT

Also by Lisa Bevere

Without Rival
Girls with Swords
Lioness Arising
Fight Like a Girl
Kissed the Girls and Made Them Cry

ADAMANT

FINDING
TRUTH
IN A UNIVERSE OF
OPINIONS

LISA BEVERE

Revell

a division of Baker Publishing Group
Grand Rapids, Michigan

© 2018 by Lisa Bevere

Published by Revell
a division of Baker Publishing Group
PO Box 6287, Grand Rapids, MI 49516-6287
www.revellbooks.com

Printed in the United States of America

Library of Congress Cataloging-in-Publication Data
Names: Bevere, Lisa, author.
Title: Adamant : finding truth in a universe of opinions / Lisa Bevere.
Description: Grand Rapids : Revell, 2018. | Includes bibliographical references and index.
Identifiers: LCCN 2017053949 | ISBN 9780800727253 (pbk. : alk. paper)
Subjects: LCSH: Christianity and culture. | Rocks—Religious aspects.
Classification: LCC BR115.C8 B424 2018 | DDC 261—dc23
LC record available at https://lccn.loc.gov/2017053949

Published in association with the Fedd Agency.

18 19 20 21 22 23 24   7 6 5 4 3 2 1

CONTENTS

ACKNOWLEDGMENTS

Rabbi Brian Bileci: thank you for your rabbinical and prophetic insight.

Scott Lindsey of Faithlife: you always help me be smart.

Andrea Doering: working with you is a dream.

Team Messenger International: I couldn't do any of this without you.

THE ADAMANT

Look to the rock from which you were hewn, and
the quarry from which you were dug.

Isaiah 51:1

For more than a year, I have pondered this verse and found myself captivated by the concept of this rock, this stone, this . . . *adamant*.

We know the word to mean immovable, impervious, and unyielding in opinion or position. And as such, the word *adamant* has gained a reputation for more than its fair share of stubbornness. But the adjectives and the adverbs we commonly associate with the term *adamant* are not the original meaning of the word. Adamant began as a noun and in so many ways as a dream.

The concept of adamant has a rather ancient and mythical history. Adamant was first known as a stone. Correction: as an unknown stone. It represented an elusive mineral whose existence was hypothesized in ancient Greece. It was there that mathematicians, philosophers, and mystics first imagined the existence of a rock like none other, a stone woven so tightly that it would be simultaneously impenetrable and unbreakable. Void of fractures or fragments, it would be hard beyond measure and yet . . . irresistible.

This stone would have the singular ability to attract and repel objects. It would draw but not be drawn, be magnetic yet immovable. The stone would have a unique relationship with light. It would be capable of gathering rays, focusing them, and redirecting their radiance. Fire would not be able to penetrate its shell, and once drawn from the flames, the rock would be cool to the touch.

These are but a few of the traits theorized about this adamant ore. The troublesome part was the matter of discovering it. Would it be found in the dark heart of the earth? Were these stones born of fire and released from the belly of a volcano? Or were these stones of wonder hidden in the depths of the sea? Would the gods award them as a gift of merit?

The Greeks named the obscure stone *adamas*, which is best translated "invincible." And even though there was not a shred of proof that adamas existed, they dreamed of ways this invincible stone could be put to use.

Weapons would be forged out of this mineral. Adamas would birth swords, axes, and knives that would not break in battle and shields that would not yield. The slenderest arrowhead fashioned of adamas would penetrate the most formidable target with ease. What of armor? Warriors cloaked in the impenetrable armor of adamas would be rendered invincible. Darkness would not stop them, for the rays captured by adamas would blind their enemies even as the stone lit their way to victory.

The belief in this rock was so compelling that the theory of its existence spread northward through Europe until it reached the shores of Great Britain. It was there that the Greek word *adamas* became the word we know, *adamant*. And there the word waited to be revealed.

With the discovery of diamonds around 400 BC in India, it was thought that man had finally found the long-sought adamant. No other stone's strength compared with that of the diamond. Every rock born of inferior fire fragmented under the force of the diamond adamant. These gems were born in wombs of such intense fire and pressure that all lesser components were consumed and what remained was a singular element: carbon, bound in the crystalline form of a diamond.

For centuries, the words *adamant* and *diamond* were used interchangeably to describe all that was invincible, immovable, and indestructible. Both the prince of preachers, Charles Spurgeon, and Puritan legend John Bunyan echoed the words of the prophet Zechariah when he bemoaned the condition of adamant hearts impervious to the Word of God and harder than flint:

> Yea, they made their hearts as an *adamant* stone, lest they should hear the law, and the words which the LORD of hosts hath sent in his spirit by the former prophets: therefore came a great wrath from the LORD of hosts. (Zech. 7:12 KJV)

More contemporary translations of this passage replaced the word *adamant* with the word *diamond*:

> They made their hearts *diamond*-hard lest they should hear the law and the words that the LORD of hosts had sent by his Spirit through the former prophets. Therefore great anger came from the LORD of hosts.

It wasn't until the late 1700s that French scientist Antoine Lavoisier discovered that, given enough heat and oxygen, diamonds would actually evaporate. With this revelation, the words *diamond* and *adamant* were disassociated, and the search for the indestructible, immovable, invincible adamant faded. The word remained as a descriptor of what was never a reality. But men dreamed. The revered Arkenstone found in the writings of J. R. R. Tolkien seems a nod to the mythical origin of the adamant. For more than two millennia, people searched for and failed to find the adamant. And yet I wonder . . .

What was the origin of this quest? Was this concept of the adamant a seed of inspiration planted by God? Why dream of what no one had yet seen, and why refer to the unknown? Or is this stone among us and unrecognized? Perhaps the adamant was never meant to be an implement of war and destruction but one of refuge and provision. Shouldn't the stone we seek welcome all? Could the purpose of the adamant be to mine what is hidden within us? In a world where truth slips and slides according to the latest popular trend and current culture, wouldn't it be nice to have something that was constant?

Immovable?

Invincible?

Unchanging?

> Could the purpose of the adamant be to mine what is hidden within us?

Perhaps these musings are nothing more than silly questions about a nonexistent stone. After all, we live in a time when no one goes on quests for stones of power. We are realists who have learned that stars are nothing more than luminous vapor. We have walked upon the barren moon and sent probes into the deep, dark caverns of the ocean floor. We have demystified much of what once inspired wonder.

And yet, stripped of our awe, we find ourselves clothed in confusion and comparison.

The highly educated often lack both purpose and opportunities.

We have bound ourselves to monetary systems of credit designed to entrap in debt those who purchase.

The political system created by our forefathers to unite the people now divides us.

Our networks are vast, but our connections are shallow and void of true intimacy.

We have chosen to become what we do and yet remain unfulfilled.

We use technology to throw stones at people we will never see.

When truth becomes fluid, we lose contact with answers larger than ourselves.

Real truth is a rock. Adamant. Indivisible. Immovable. Invincible.

Jesus is truth. And I propose that Jesus is the Adamant.

Jesus the Adamant

No stone born of earth can stand before the living Stone. In Christ, all that the Greeks and the mystics looked for was realized. He is our Rock, our Cornerstone, and our long-awaited Adamant. Christ alone is the unchanging Stone with the power to change everything. And long has the Rock of Ages been among us. As the children of Israel wandered the desert in what seemed to be an aimless pursuit, Moses declared the presence of this Rock:

> The Rock, his work is perfect,
>> for all his ways are justice.
> A God of faithfulness and without iniquity,
>> just and upright is he. (Deut. 32:4)

And after a season in the wilderness, David cried out to God on the day of his deliverance:

> I love you, O Lord, my strength.
>> The Lord is my rock and my fortress and my
>> deliverer,
> my God, my rock, in whom I take refuge,
>> my shield, and the horn of my salvation, my
>> stronghold. (Ps. 18:1–2)

The Old Testament Hebrew word used here for *rock* means "the inaccessible refuge." The Rock is our strength, our sure footing in a world littered with gravel. Jesus is our stronghold when our enemies want to put us in a stranglehold. The Rock is our rescue, safeguard, and armor of defense. Christ anoints us with the oil of his Spirit and declares his salvation to our detractors.

In so many ways, we are all refugees on this earth looking for that high, secure, and sacred place. We long for the safety of a realm ruled by untainted justice. Like the Israelites, we have left behind our Egyptian taskmasters, but we have yet to master the enslaving voices that their cruelty imprinted on us. Even so, the Rock accompanied us as we wandered in wildernesses of purpose and preparation, but we knew it not. It is time we acknowledge our brokenness and fall again upon the Rock that we might be mended.

> And the one who falls on this stone will be broken to pieces; and when it falls on anyone, it will crush him. (Matt. 21:44)

This verse refers to Jesus, who is both the Stone and the Son. Both were rejected by man though authored by God. The Son was the Stone that came to crush the oppressive kingdoms of man and act as the Cornerstone that establishes the kingdom of God. N. T. Wright highlights this profound connection:

> And—just as in English the letters of the word "Son" are the same as the letters of the word "Stone," with two more added, so in Hebrew, by coincidence, the letters of the word *ben* (son) are the same as those of the word *eben* (stone), with one more added.[1]

I am so thankful that in Christ we were added to both the Stone and the Son. In Christ, the isolated find their home and the many become one. Christ is the Stone fashioned from the mountain of God yet untouched by human hands. He is the Rock before which no earthly kingdom can stand. Daniel prophesied this confrontation with Christ our Adamant when he described both the hidden dream and the interpretation of the dream to King Nebuchadnezzar:

> In Christ, the isolated find their home and the many become one.

> You saw, O king, and behold, a great image. This image, mighty and of exceeding brightness, stood before you, and its appearance was frightening. The head of this image was of fine gold, its chest and arms of silver, its middle and thighs of bronze,

its legs of iron, its feet partly of iron and partly of clay. As you looked, a stone was cut out by no human hand, and it struck the image on its feet of iron and clay, and broke them in pieces. Then the iron, the clay, the bronze, the silver, and the gold, all together were broken in pieces, and became like the chaff of the summer threshing floors, and the wind carried them away, so that not a trace of them could be found. *But the stone that struck the image became a great mountain and filled the whole earth.* (Dan. 2:31–35)

In Christ, a seed became a stone, and the stone grew into a mountain. The mountain that filled the whole earth is Zion, and the seed stone of this mountain is Christ. If we foolishly attempt to build our lives with the very materials that cannot stand the blow of the Stone, our pursuits will be shattered then scattered, blown by the winds of time. Jesus shakes all that can be shaken so that only the unshakable and true remain. Embrace the trembling, my friend. Let your heart quake, for he loves you far too much to allow you to be ensnared in half-truths and faulty kingdom foundations once again. You were never meant to build with earthbound metals and soil. You were made to be a living stone.

> Let your heart quake, for he loves you far too much to allow you to be ensnared in half-truths.

Living Stones

As you come to him, a living stone rejected by men but in the sight of God chosen and precious, you yourselves like living stones are being built up as a spiritual house, to be a holy priesthood, to offer spiritual sacrifices acceptable to God through Jesus Christ. (1 Pet. 2:4–5)

In the Message translation, this passage begins with "Welcome to the living Stone, the source of life." In Christ, our hearts come alive, and we too become living stones, set in the body to realize our purposes. We are here to offer our lives in the service of building a spiritual house or sanctuary. We do not hold the role of builder. We are the raw material Christ uses to construct his church.

I love the word *sanctuary*. It is a preserve or shelter, a haven of safety, protection, and immunity. What a picture of our lives as adamants of safety! This is not a dead building. It is a refuge, vibrant with life, where we offer our Father our lives, just as the priests of the temple did. Peter continues this image in 1 Peter 2:6–8:

For it stands in Scripture: "Behold, I am laying in Zion a stone, a cornerstone chosen and precious, and whoever believes in him will not be put to shame." So the honor is for you who believe, but for those who do not believe, "The stone that the builders rejected has become the cornerstone," and "A stone of stumbling, and a rock of offense." They stumble because they disobey the word, as they were destined to do.

I know sometimes things are said and done that make us want to go quiet about the fact that we are churchgoing Christians, but never for a minute should we be ashamed of our Cornerstone. Jesus is flawless. We are flawed diamonds that often diminish his radiance with our inclusions, but our Master Builder weaves us together so that the best of each of us is magnified and the flaws are redeemed.

People fail us.

People fail to see us.

We fail people and fail to see each other the way Jesus sees us.

But for all our days, we must honor Jesus, for he never disappoints. He was tested without faltering or failing. Jesus is committed to loving his flawed bride, the church, into radiance and readiness. Shouldn't we do the same?

In the book of Isaiah, we read:

> Therefore thus says the Lord GOD, "Behold, I am the one who has laid as a foundation in Zion, a stone, a tested stone, a precious cornerstone, of a sure foundation: 'Whoever believes will not be in haste.'" (28:16)

> **Jesus is committed to loving his flawed bride, the church, into radiance and readiness.**

The Hebrew word for *haste* means more than hurried—it also means "to be agitated and disturbed." That's a promise to us—to you and to me: we who believe will not be agitated or disturbed. We will be kept in perfect peace as our minds are stayed on our adamant Cornerstone (Isa. 26:3).

With Jesus, the focus shifted, and the cast-aside one (Jesus) became a home for the outcast.

> But you are a chosen race, a royal priesthood, a holy nation, a people for his own possession, that you may proclaim the excellencies of him who called you out of darkness into his marvelous light. Once you were not a people, but now you are God's people; once you had not received mercy, but now you have received mercy. (1 Pet. 2:9–10)

Once we were not his; now we are. Once we were rejected; now we are accepted. Once we were divided; now in Christ we are one.

But you . . . but me . . . but we the many outsiders . . . were chosen by God and called to the priestly work of a holy people. We give witness to what he has done in our lives. His new is exchanged for our old, and our death is exchanged for his life. We embrace the Stone and cry out from the pile of our broken pieces by inviting our Cornerstone to make us whole. In Christ, we have gone from the rejected to the accepted. In him, we who were *nothing* got in on *everything*.

In him, we who were *nothing* got in on *everything*.

Our Cornerstone is not a buried remnant of the past. Jesus is not a dead stone mined from the depths of the molten earth. Christ is the living Stone and as such the architect of our new beginning. He is an unchanging Stone with the power to change us.

Stones and Seeds

In ancient architecture, the cornerstone was considered *the seed* from which the entire building would germinate. The cornerstone began the pattern that every other stone would follow. It was so important that the cornerstone be precisely set in place that builders would use the stars to align the cornerstone with the points of a compass. How beautiful that the stars declared the coming of our Cornerstone.

Our modern architecture no longer uses the cornerstone as the seed of a building. Our cornerstones are merely decorative plaques added on after the building is complete to commemorate the date it was established. These cornerstones serve no structural purpose; they are simply a commemorative add-on. Conversely, Jesus is not a decorative add-on to our lives. He is our pattern and the seed from which our entire lives will come.

Not only is he our refuge and the seed of our foundation, but he is also our refreshing.

With the coming of Jesus Christ, Paul explains the Rock of Exodus to the church at Corinth: "For they drank from the spiritual Rock that followed them, and the Rock was Christ" (1 Cor. 10:4). As the Israelites followed Moses through the desert, they were refreshed by water from a rock—a rock that followed them. Christ was that Rock. Even then, the tender love and provision of God was present, and Jesus was their rearguard.

How curious.

This stone not only provided water for millions but also moved along with them. God appeared as a pillar of cloud by day, a pillar of fire by night, and both day and night the rock that followed. This is such a beautiful picture of God's ever-present care for the children of Israel as they traveled through the wilderness. Some rabbinic traditions say this was an actual rock that resembled a sieve, which rolled along with them and came to rest at the tent of meeting when they settled.[2]

Whether this wilderness rock literally or figuratively followed them, Paul is saying this rock represented the preexistent Christ, their ever-present rearguard. The rock foreshadowed Emmanuel, our always present Lord. Even now Christ is the Rock who travels with us through the wildernesses of life, refreshing us with living water.

He opened the rock, and water gushed out;
it flowed through the desert like a river.
(Ps. 105:41)

Life can be riddled with desert seasons, and deserts have a way of revealing our source of life. Some arid seasons last weeks, others months, and then there are those that stretch their parched hands over years. But no matter how desolate your current surroundings may seem or how long they last, there is a river hidden within your wilderness. This river is not around you; it is within you. If you are thirsty, if your life is desolate, cry out to the Rock.

On the cross, this Rock, Jesus, was opened once again, and this time blood and water flowed from his side . . . water to wash and blood to redeem.

The goodness of our Rock is impervious to our awfulness. As our Adamant encounters our flaws, they become as dust in the presence of his perfection. It is not that he is unaware of our violations. He sees the pain and shame that our willful choices bring upon ourselves and others. It is just that he cannot help but be what he is . . . good and merciful. He is the Lord and Savior of all, and any who throw their broken lives on his adamant mercy are transformed.

> He cannot help but be what he is . . . good and merciful.

A New Name

And Jesus answered him, "Blessed are you, Simon Bar-Jonah! For flesh and blood has not revealed this to you, but my Father who is in heaven. And I tell you, *you are Peter*, and on this rock I will build my church, and the gates of hell shall not prevail against it. (Matt. 16:17–18)

"You are Peter."

New life requires a renewed nature. A new nature requires the gift of a new name.

This declaration must have reverberated deep within Simon's soul. What must it have felt like to be singled out and called a rock after he'd spent his entire life known by a very different name?

Simon. There was nothing wrong with this name. It just wasn't big enough. It spoke of who he had been rather than who he was becoming. When we speak and say something different, we begin to see differently. Peter was the new name that fit his divine destiny.

Simon means "to listen and to hear." It can also mean "reed-like and pliable in nature." When we weave these two together, we find a name that could mean one who is bent in the direction of what they hear and listen to. In that light, we are all Simons, waiting to be renamed in the light of our destiny, for like him we tend to move in the direction of what we hear.

In this conversation with Simon, the name change foreshadowed our position in Christ, for he changes each of us from a swaying reed to a rampart of adamant.

Simon needed to transition from a fisherman to a fisher of men. The renaming of Simon closed the pages of an old book so God could take pen and paper in hand to write a new one.

I wonder if the name Peter felt odd at first. Or was it the name he had longed to be called all his life? Will the same be true for us? Did you know that in heaven we will all receive a stone with our truest name on it? Jesus promised:

To the one who conquers I will give some of the hidden manna, and I will give him *a white stone, with a new name written on the stone that no one knows except the one who receives it.* (Rev. 2:17)

This new name declares victories. It is etched with how we conquered our fears and became who God created us to be. I find it fascinating that our new name is written in stone. To me this says that who we have been is in flux, but who we are becoming is eternal. Why would I choose to live in the confines of a name that fits my *now* when my Rock is fashioning one for me that will fit forever? I am alive to grow into the likeness of my new name.

Something shifts when what Jesus says about us becomes a part of us. In those moments, we glimpse a fraction of what it means to know as we are known. This is one of the many reasons why I love that it is Peter the rock who welcomes us to our Cornerstone.

> I am alive to grow into the likeness of my new name.

This isn't the first time that Jesus worked with stone. When we think of carpenters, we think of those who work with wood, but in Jesus's day, carpenters were also "artificers in stone, iron and copper, as well as in wood."[3] Our Cornerstone was familiar with stones.

On earth, we are known by the name given by our parents. In eternity, we will have a new name known only to us. Until that time when the unknown is made known to us, we have the privilege of living in the wonder of the name of Jesus.

In Christ, rocks join together to form a holy mountain.

In Christ, small seeds grow into large trees.

In Christ, hearts of rock become living stones.
In Christ, the many become one.

Secure in Him

Our position in Christ is not based on our ability to hold on. The moment we hide ourselves in him, we are secured in his ability to hold us. In Christ, our Rock, our Adamant, our Cornerstone, we are safe.

Recently, I flew into Chicago, and on the hour-long taxi ride to my hotel, my Muslim driver tried to convert me to Islam. He assured me that if I prayed every day and lived according to the tenets of Islam, there would be a chance I'd make it to paradise. It was a definite maybe. No guarantee, but there was a chance. He kindly offered me a place on a rock, with no promise. I was painfully aware that I could slip and fall off this rock. I choose to remain in Christ; I will fall but never outside of him.

We fall in him not off him.

In order that we might abide *in him*, God places a measure of his faith *in us*. We stumble when we place our faith in someone. We will never falter when our faith is in God. Let the faith of God have entrance in your life. Invite it in. You have tried and failed in your own strength. You have watched as others have faltered as they attempted to climb the scree-strewn rock of faith in the strength of self. Just because faith is unseen doesn't mean it doesn't exist or it won't happen. Faith is the hidden quickening of hope that leaps within us to help us believe there can be more. Faith gives us the courage to ask for more, to dare to dream that in Christ we too can be adamant, immovable, and invincible.

Mountains

We are invited to climb the mountains of our lives by God's strength, following in his footprints. Recently, I wrote this in my journal:

> They call to me, these mountain heights, oh come away and be my delight. They lure me with mysteries beyond compare, known only by those who dare. But I am old and not as strong. Why did your call wait so long? He answered, "Yes, the climb is steep, but I am strong. Your youth renews as you follow the path I've set you on."

I live in Colorado with a view of the mountains all day long. So for me, God's whisper to follow him to the mountain makes sense. I don't know the geography of where you live, but know this—you have been invited to the ascent as well. Not to Sinai the stony mountain, whose very base could not be touched. You have been welcomed to Zion, a living mountain of wonder.

> But you have come to Mount Zion and to the city of the living God, the heavenly Jerusalem, and to innumerable angels in festal gathering, and to the assembly of the firstborn who are enrolled in heaven, and to God, the judge of all, and to the spirits of the righteous made perfect, and to Jesus, the mediator of a new covenant, and to the sprinkled blood that speaks a better word than the blood of Abel. (Heb. 12:22–24)

Something happens as we step into the wonder of this invitation.

John Muir, the respected naturalist who championed the need for wild spaces, once said, "We are now in the mountains and they are in us, kindling enthusiasm, making every nerve quiver, filling every pore and cell of us."[4] These words were penned to describe the wonder of the Sierra Nevada Mountains, an earthly range covered with nature and wildlife. How much more could this be said of a living mountain we could enter even as it enters us? For not only are we in Christ . . . but Christ is also the hope within us. Our hope comes from the Mount of Zion, even as we invite his reign within us.

May these pages serve as a welcome to all who have ever felt rejected and as a refuge to all who quake with fear. As you journey, may you enter into the wonder and solidarity of truth and escape the snare of confusion and earthbound opinions. Our Adamant has not moved; he has ever been with us.

Dear heavenly Father,
I choose to embrace all that it means to be a living
stone and a royal priest. Be my refuge and my strength,
my refreshing and my hope. Etch the name you have
given me upon my heart. Christ, my Cornerstone and
Adamant, the unmovable and invincible source of life,
I fall upon you. Have your way in my life.

2

ADAMANTLY INTIMATE

> We are not human beings having a spiritual experience. We are spiritual beings having a human experience.
>
> Pierre Teilhard de Chardin

I was not an easy child. I was strong-willed and stubborn. I could also be melancholy, withdrawn, and easily distracted. If I was sent to my room to clean it, in a matter of minutes, I would forget why I was there. When my door closed, I turned on my music and my imagination took over. Rather than straighten my room, I might rearrange my furniture. At other times, I donned a sunbonnet and pretended I was Laura Ingalls Wilder. In a drawer, there was a blue block of clay begging me to sculpt a horse, or there were the dolls my grandmother had brought me from faraway lands that wanted rearranging. And there were always books demanding my attention. In my room, I lost all sense of time. An hour felt like fifteen minutes.

It wasn't until I heard my mother calling my name that I'd remember I had been sent to my room for a reason. But I just could not remember what it was. So when my mother checked on me, there was no evidence of progress. Rather, the room had grown worse rather than better.

It wasn't that I meant to disobey, but somehow I always did. This pattern of behavior understandably frustrated my mother to no end. I would try to counter her anger by drawing her into my world of pretend, but my mother was living in a very real nightmare she couldn't escape. She was caught in the cycle of chaos that only someone married to an adulterer and an alcoholic would understand.

Because I was the oldest and the only daughter, her anger was vented on me. In so many ways, I looked and acted like my father. She said many things she probably never meant and did things she would have gladly taken back—things so long ago forgiven they are not worth repeating. But the words that passed between us and the things that were done made me never want a daughter. I share this only so you can understand how beautiful the encounter I had with Jesus really was.

When I was pregnant for the fourth time, many assumed the child would be a girl. I mean, who has four boys in a row . . . right? It was early in my pregnancy, and I was wrestling with the fear that the birth of a daughter might be imminent.

So many times my mother had scolded me with, "I hope you have a daughter just like you!"

And so many times I had defiantly countered, "I hope I do too!"

Maybe at one point those words had been true, but as time passed, they became a lie. I didn't want that daughter, not even a little bit. I was already overwhelmed with a husband who traveled all the time and three young sons. What would adding a daughter into our crazy mix look like? I didn't know how to do girl!

In a time of prayer, I got gut-level honest with God.

In whispered tones, I voiced each of the fears that stormed through my head. I let him know that giving me a daughter would be a big mistake. I didn't want to hurt her like my mother had hurt me and her mother had hurt her. I was afraid I wouldn't bond with her. In my willful youth, I had said things I didn't mean. I didn't want a daughter like me.

After a while, my torrent of words ran dry and a sense of stillness settled over me. My eyes were closed as I took a deep breath and let it out.

In my mind's eye, I saw myself at the edge of a wide-open meadow where flowers and emerald grass swayed in the light of golden sunshine. It was the type of field that invites you to run through it. In the distance was a single tower. I felt compelled to go to it. The tower had a single entrance and was wrapped with tall, narrow windows that made their way upward in a spiral. (I know now they were arrow slits.) I opened the door. The interior was dim in contrast with the bright sunshine, but not dark or foreboding. The windows revealed a staircase that wound upwards. I climbed the stairs, pausing at each window. As far as I could see, there were neither people nor houses. Each opening gave me a view of another portion of the meadow.

When I reached the top of the stairs, I found a round room with windows under the eaves. The far wall sheltered a large wooden chest. I wanted to look inside it. I expected it to hold weapons, supplies, or possibly even treasure of some sort. I knelt on the floor and lifted the unlocked lid. What I found astounded me. The chest was filled with photos of me as a child.

There were pictures of me with missing teeth. Photos of me before and after my eye had been removed. Photos of summer holidays, Christmases, birthdays, and my parents smiling. I held in my hands all the pictures that had been lost decades earlier when our basement had flooded. Here they were in a watchtower, safely hidden away in a treasure chest. Caught up in this joy of recovery, I held one up for a closer look. I was probably no more than five, my face and hair full of sunshine. I was squinting like Popeye and flashing my father a crooked smile as he captured the moment. I can still see it.

> The love of God hovered over me as I wept like a baby.

My reverie was interrupted when I heard a man's voice say, "I always thought you were funny."

I turned, but Jesus was not there. I knew it was he who spoke because the warmth of his tangible presence lingered. The love of God hovered over me as I wept like a baby.

In that single moment, every word that had ever been spoken that caused me to see myself as an awful child took flight like a winged bird. How poignant that these images were kept in an armory, for they were intimate weapons of healing.

Intimate

Our God is adamantly intimate. He knew my fears and spoke directly into my spirit. That is how he wants to speak to you as well. He remembers those moments that made him smile, the very ones we have forgotten. He has forgotten our sin and shame and buried our transgressions in a sea of forgetfulness. He draws us near to heal and mend.

We lose sight of our identities when we attach them to the wrong imagery. We lose our abilities when we allow fear and even the pain of others to bury our gifts. But we can run and hide in him, and he will speak truth to the most intimate places of our hearts. He longs to rock the rejected in his arms and then plant us in his truth.

I hope you already know this:

You are so much more than what you or others can see or touch.

You are so much more than what you've known or done.

You are so much more than what others think or even how your perceptions frame your self-image.

You could never be accurately measured by what you own or lack.

You are more than the span of your years and therefore cannot be tethered to the adages of young or old.

You are a child of the eternal realm.

You are more than single, divorced, widowed, or married.

You are far more than your gender.

These attributes are tangible expressions of the structure that houses the real life that is you. They are relational dynamics and material possessions. They are like pieces of clothing that cover us and the bodies that shelter us. They represent how our lives appear to be, but they are not our source of life.

If a fire ravaged my house and consumed all of its contents but I escaped through a veil of the flames, my life would be intact.

Spirit

I am a living spirit.
You are a living spirit.
We were created in the image of God, and God is spirit. Though it is invisible, this spirit is as real and as near as the very breath we draw. And yet it is something deeper than the passage of air through our lungs. It is the quickening of God dwelling within us. The God of fire and love consumes all that hinders the expression and reception of his love.

God is spirit, and those who worship him must worship in spirit and truth. (John 4:24)

God is spirit. God is truth. Therefore, we worship him both in spirit and in truth.

Presently, the flawed confines of our human frames are an awkward fit for our spirits. The tension between our longing for release and the reality of our earthly containment is often the very thing that awakens a desire for more.

When we were young, this frustration urged us to grow. That thing just beyond our reach is what drove us to roll or crawl. After a while, movement alone was not enough. Why spend our days looking at the floor? In answer, we left behind the safety and speed of crawling to pull up and stand. Standing expanded our view, and for a short season, we were content to drop back on our bottoms to move. But there came a day when standing on two legs and then dropping back to all fours was no longer enough. We lifted our heads to walk erect.

Young and old, we are frustrated by limits and betrayed by the same. So why would any of us ever imagine that a human physical experience would have the power to heal the human spirit? Our emotions can be touched and our bodies can be pleased, but the covering of flesh cannot touch spirit.

Even though it is the very breath of God's Spirit that animates all that can be touched and gives us the capacity to feel.

And it is the spirit that quickens the body, as James says:

His voice speaks life.

> The body apart from the spirit is dead. (James 2:26)

Once the spirit has departed the body, the body is drawn back toward the realm of the earth, from which it was formed. The spirit was all that gave the body life and purpose, and with its absence, the body is compelled to decay. But there is another kind of death that James and Paul talk about—a dead faith.

> Faith apart from works is dead. (James 2:26)

> The letter kills, but the Spirit gives life. (2 Cor. 3:6)

Don't settle for religion void of God's presence or for turning the pages of the Bible without the wind of his Spirit. His voice speaks life. The limits of the letter of the law are not simply the humanly impossible legalities of religion—the law also includes what our culture has scribed on our flesh. It is the labels we are encouraged to wear.

Until we see that living by labels and letters is death, we will continue to turn to the wrong source for the right thing. We need someone to speak spirit-to-spirit to the depths of our longing and bring clarity to our human confusion. There are far too many smoke-and-mirrors games in play in our culture. People are distracted by an illusion, while an operator behind the curtain controls what we see and hear. Maybe you're hiding behind that curtain, making things appear one way when in reality you are desperate to be seen. Truly seen. Our God sees.

The God Who Hovers

In the beginning, God created the heavens and the earth. The earth was without form and void, and darkness was over the face of the deep. And the Spirit of God was hovering over the face of the waters. (Gen. 1:1–2)

From the very beginning, our God was the Creator. When the earth was held captive, shrouded in a formless void of water, and darkness which veiled the countenance of the deep . . . God drew near. Rather than turn away in disappointment or distance himself from the shapeless, barren abyss of dark water, the Spirit of God hovered.

I want to pause and paint some imagery around this word *hovering*.

The Hebrew word for *hovering*, *rachaf*, evokes such a beautiful picture and is best translated as "to linger or to float in a manner that is at once gentle and cherishing." The rabbinic notation that accompanies this word for *hovering* is "like a dove."[1]

Rachaf also means "to flutter over." The word is seen again in this reference:

> He found him in a desert land, and in the howling waste of the wilderness; he encircled him, he cared for him, he kept him as the apple of his eye. Like an eagle that stirs up its nest, *that flutters over its young*, spreading out its wings, catching them, bearing them on its pinions. (Deut. 32:10–11)

This reference compares how God protected and cared for the children of Israel to how an eagle interacts with its young. The Spirit of God hovered over them with protection as he led them from a place of desolation to a land of promise.

I can't help but imagine the tenderness of a mother as she pauses over the bed of her sleeping child tossing fretfully in the throes of a bad dream. Are we willing to be awakened?

And while the Spirit of God hovered and covered, he spoke. His words were chosen with care. He did not echo the reality of a formless, void sphere of darkness. He released what would shape what should be. In the face of chaos and darkness, God called forth an awakening. Face-to-face with the finality of dark waters, God spoke a dawn, a new beginning, a day. God spoke light.

> And God said, "Let there be light," and there was light. And God saw that the light was good. And God separated the light from the darkness. (Gen. 1:3–4)

And light appeared, and it was good. The Hebrew word for *light* here has its origin in God, which isn't surprising because God is light void of shadow. This was not the placement

—————◇————— **God is light void of shadow.**

of the sun. That event came later in creation. This light emanated from God and reached out to illuminate the dark recesses of the earth. It is one thing to have a torch in our hand and quite another to be a light source. We carry light. But God *is* light. Quickening light is in his very breath.

Therefore, he spoke his very essence into our earth, and it was good because . . . *God is good.*

The Hebrew word used here in Genesis 1 for *good* encompasses many English words: desirable, efficient, kind, moral, and increasing in value are just a few. When light was released, the earth was seeded with all of these attributes and more. This genesis positioned the earth to become an attractive, productive environment that was kind and moral to its inhabitants, and with each passing year, it would become increasingly more valuable. A pattern of the goodness of God was set in motion.

We have no sure way of knowing if this origin of earth light was an explosion or if the light levels rose slowly like the dawning of a new day. What we do know for certain is that God was the light source, the light was good, and the light was best separated from darkness.

> God called the light Day, and the darkness he called Night.
> And there was evening and there was morning, the first day.
> (Gen. 1:5)

Once light was released, things began to happen. Next God separated the waters by an expanse, thus creating the atmosphere and cushion of space that surrounds the earth. Once this protective environment was in place, things long submerged and hidden by the dark deep rose to the light and surfaced.

And God said, "Let the waters under the heavens be gathered together into one place, and let the dry land appear." And it was so. God called the dry land Earth, and the waters that were gathered together he called Seas. And God saw that it was good. (Gen. 1:9–10)

What was hidden was revealed. The land had always been there, covered by fathoms of dark water, awaiting its release. I imagine the earth held its breath and watched in hope as light appeared through the wavering waters. The land waited for the word of God to call it forth. And the land began to burst with life.

And God said, "Let the earth sprout vegetation, plants yielding seed, and fruit trees bearing fruit in which is their seed, each according to its kind, on the earth." And it was so. (Gen. 1:11)

The next day the rulers of the day and the night, the sun and the moon and the stars, were appointed. This means that all the living things were at first growing under the warmth and golden glow of the light of God. He was the light source, just as one day he will be again.

And night will be no more. They will need no light of lamp or sun, for the Lord God will be their light, and they will reign forever and ever. (Rev. 22:5)

Once the reign and the realms of the sun and the moon were established, God spoke to the domains of water and sky and called forth the fish and the flying creatures of the air. The depths of the oceans and the expanse of the sky teemed with their flitting and fluttering life. Where the Spirit of God had once hovered, now creatures flew. The following day was set aside for the life that roamed the land.

> And God said, "Let the earth bring forth living creatures according to their kinds—livestock and creeping things and beasts of the earth according to their kinds." And it was so. (Gen. 1:24)

The sea, the air, and the earth had each brought forth according to its kind and nature. It was time the Creator brought forth according to his.

> So God created man in his own image, in the image of God he created him; male and female he created them. (Gen. 1:27)

Humankind was created in his image. I wonder if we understand the privilege of being formed as a reflection of our masterful Creator.

Before the fall, we can only guess at the magnificence of each creature. And yet they cannot approach the image of God woven within you. I'm not just saying this. I know it to be true. You doubt it because you cannot actually see who you really are. Man and woman were created magnificent.

> Then the LORD God formed the man of dust from the ground and breathed into his nostrils the breath of life, and the man became a living creature. (Gen. 2:7)

First God formed, then God breathed. Using the dust of this light-quickened realm, the Creator gave man the capacity to contain his very own breath. The I Am Who I Am breathed his life into the shape of a man, and what was a shell came alive. When Adam was first created, he was whole. He was perfect in physical form, and man's spirit and soul were unified. Adam and Eve were perfect.

Don't be frightened by what I have just said. Don't let it puff you up with arrogance either. Allow the royal designation of God's original intent for us to be image bearers of the Most High God to place its weight upon your shoulders. In the trespass of Adam and Eve, we toppled further than we could ever retrieve ourselves. Now, hidden within our invincible refuge, Christ our Cornerstone, we dimly reflect what we had been and wait for the glorious hope of what we one day will be. As C. S. Lewis so aptly noted:

> "You come of the Lord Adam and the Lady Eve," said Aslan. "And that is both honour enough to erect the head of the poorest beggar, and shame enough to bow the shoulders of the greatest emperor on earth. Be content."[2]

You were made for intimate, spirit-filled connection with the Father.

We are children of soil formed from the dust of the earth long after the fall had its way with our world. Our spirits came alive when we were born again, but our minds and bodies are in need of sanctuary and renewal.

> He reveals deep and hidden things;
> he knows what is in the darkness,
> and the light dwells with him. (Dan. 2:22)

In the trespass of Adam and Eve, we toppled further than we could ever retrieve ourselves.

In the fall this intimate weaving of the soul and spirit was rent. To understand this better it could be likened to a vessel that is present but no longer full. Even though it is his breath that sustains our frame, we carry an awareness of our gap, our void. We breathe because he is, but the shallowness of each breath says there is more because it doesn't fill us. Without *God's* spirit we live as those who are on life support.

Now I must share why I have taken the time and space to unpack the creation account in this manner for you. I have a sense that the Spirit of God wants to hover over some areas in your life. He wants to do a Genesis makeover. He wants to:

quicken you with his light (2 Cor. 4:6)

separate light from darkness (2 Cor. 6:14)

create a canopy of expanse over your life (Rom. 4:7–8)

roll back the dark blanket of water and reveal the new ground (Heb. 11:29)

release the seeds buried within your soil so they may sprout and bring forth fruit (Mark 4:20)

call forth life and wonder in your deep waters (John 7:38)

free your heart from fear so it can take flight in faith (Matt. 6:22; Mark 6:50)

astound you with the creativity of his vast creation (Ps. 19:1–6)

breathe life, his life, into the cavity created by sin, reweave your spirit and soul and heal all that has been torn and rent (John 20:21–22; Col. 2:2)

Even now our Creator longs to draw near and come face-to-face with any place veiled in darkness or misty confusion and shed his light. His Spirit hovers over the formless, voided places in our lives. He is not ignorant of our pain or repulsed by our condition. He sees us wrestling with confusion. He does not pull away when he sees us struggling. His Spirit draws near, waiting, lingering, oh so gently, like a mother beside a frightened or fitful child, like an eagle fluttering over a nest of baby birds as they hatch, watching expectantly as they escape the confines of their thin shells. Later, the eagle will hover again as they learn to

> Intimacy leaves no room for shadowed spaces.

fly. This is the adamantly intimate, steadfast nature of our Creator, who is at once around us and within us. Intimacy leaves no room for shadowed spaces, so do not hide. Your Father sees and loves the real you. Trust that the one who formed you will also breathe his life into you.

Intimacy Brings Wholeness

One thing God cannot do is lie.

He will not repeat the lies others have spoken over you.

He will not allow a lie you've spoken over yourself to be called truth.

He will not allow a label to be your limit. In his presence, every label falls away, even the ones you've written on yourself.

He calls you by name, not the names you've been called.

He calls you by the name the Spirit sees when it hovers.

He's been face-to-face with your deepest longings and darkest fears.

He sees the unformed places.

He sees the disappointed hope.

He sees the misty clouds of confusion.

He sees the heaving tumult of humanity in crisis.

He hears the cries of the frightened and the lonely.

He feels the pain of the shunned and the isolated.

He sees the snare of sin and shame.

He sees the many waters that threaten to overwhelm.

He sees through the fathoms of darkness that grayed the color of your world with swaths of shadow.

He sees all of this and speaks light.

Others may call you girl. He calls you daughter.

Others may call you a failure. He calls you daughter.

You may call yourself heterosexual, transgender, asexual, lesbian, or any other of a vast assortment of labels. He calls you his own.

Daughter is higher and reaches deeper than gender.

Daughter is more intimate than your sexual orientation.

Daughter is who you are to your Creator.

God doesn't address us as girls and boys.

He calls us daughters and sons.

There are intimate places in each of us that can be touched only by him. There are places within us that were created to respond to God's Spirit. We call out for his touch each time we breathe the name of Jesus.

I don't know if our planet cried out when it was submerged in the depths of a watery grave. I don't know why the Spirit of God chose then to hover. I do know that now the Spirit of God is as close to us as a whisper, waiting to encircle us and gather us close.

In the New Testament, the heart of the Creator was echoed in the words of Jesus:

O Jerusalem, Jerusalem, the city that kills the prophets and stones those who are sent to it! How often would I have gathered your children together as a hen gathers her brood under her wings, and you were not willing! (Matt. 23:37)

How tragic are the words "you were not willing."

Even now the Spirit of God hovers, waiting to speak peace to the storms and to silence the cries of our howling wastelands. He waits, longing to encircle us with the protection and warmth of his wings. Are we willing? Will we invite the Holy Spirit who hovers to draw near? Will we allow him to cover us? Will we persist with our attempts to cover ourselves even as we uncover others? Will we listen to our Creator?

Intimacy is part of our deep and desperate human desire to simply belong.

We long to belong . . . because we were created to belong.

We crave intimacy . . . because we were created for intimacy.

We need to love and be loved . . . because we were created for love.

And we were created by love.

The truth is we tend to oversimplify some things and complicate others. When it comes to gender, we do both. I live in a woman's body, but ultimately I am a spirit. We are all spiritual beings having a rather rough human experience. This earth is not our home, so it shouldn't surprise us that at times our bodies feel awkward, limiting, and constrictive. They will never feel otherwise until our mortal, corruptible frames put on their immortal bodies. We are seeds awaiting release. Then and only then will we discover who and what we really are.

We are all broken. Belonging to other broken people will not fix our brokenness any more than having sex will fulfill our longing for intimacy. If it did, prostitutes and sex addicts would be the most fulfilled people on the planet. (I think we all agree that's not the case.) But there is One to whom we belong, One who can heal our brokenness and fulfill our need for intimacy. It is the Spirit of God who hovers and makes us once again whole.

Remember the verse in Daniel 2, where the stone untouched by human hands becomes the mountain? This concept is echoed in the book of Isaiah:

> There's a day coming when the mountain of GOD's House will be The Mountain—solid, towering over all mountains. All nations will river toward it, people from all over set out for it. They'll say, "Come, let's climb GOD's Mountain, go to the House of the God of Jacob. *He'll show us the way he works so we can live the way we're made.*" Zion's the source of the revelation. GOD's Message comes from Jerusalem. (2:2–3 Message)

God will show us the way he works so we can live the way we're made. We were made for immovable, invincible intimacy that will not be dissuaded by our deepest longings or put off by our most primal fears. If we ask, he will show us the light of his goodness. Pause, ponder, and allow his light to quicken you.

Dear heavenly Father,
I dare to believe that you are not distant or disapproving; you are near. There are things immersed in the deep waters of my life that I can no longer see. I give you permission to speak into my life. Release your light

and separate it from any darkness and confusion in my life. I receive your designation of daughter. Show me the way you are working in my life so I can live the way I was made . . . for your glory. In the name of Jesus, amen.

3

ADAMANTLY CONSTANT

Jesus Christ is the same yesterday and today and
forever.

Hebrews 13:8

In my life, a weekend off is a rarity. A weekend alone is
a wonder.

Even so, I admit I've been hiding. Did I hear you ask
from what?

Well, this book actually.

It's not merely procrastination that has me stymied, though
I admit it is a skill I have managed to excel at. No, I am
daunted by something far more intimidating than a deadline.

I am not sure I have ever felt such a need *for* or the weight
of a message. I feel such a sense of urgency not only to find
the right words but also to scribe these words with the right
tone. It is my earnest prayer that once both words and Scriptures are found, they will be assembled in such a way that

they are not only read . . . but also received from a friend and mother who wants you to know that you are loved beyond imagination and measure.

Today I begin again to tackle what I have touched and drawn back from multiple times. I am alone with my laptop, and there is no meeting, no event to hide behind. It is Saturday, my office is closed, and I am away from home for the sole purpose of writing. Earlier in the morning, I rode my bike to the farmers' market to stock up on good, fresh food for the next few days. I am armed with a fresh, crusty loaf of Parmesan thyme bread. I will begin with what I have been hearing in my spirit all morning: "I am the Lord, thy God, I change not."

God doesn't change. He doesn't need to change.

I woke to these words. All morning this declaration echoed within the walls of my mind. Finally, I wrote it down in my journal. Usually, once something is recorded and thus acknowledged, the persistence is silenced. But today capturing the words did not render them mute. I looked for this phrase in Scripture. I found its closest counterpart in Malachi: "For I the LORD do not change; therefore you, O children of Jacob, are not consumed" (3:6).

I broke this sentence into phrases and pieces while I sat outside devouring nearly half the loaf.

The first words I examined were the last ones I heard: "I change not."

God doesn't change. He doesn't need to change. He is committed. He is all in. His response to us is based on who he is rather than who we are or are not. Thank God, because if God changed, we would all be in trouble.

It is comforting to know that God does not change and rather alarming to realize that if he did . . . it would mean our utter destruction.

Malachi is the last book of the Old Testament. This verse comes on the heels of the first five verses of chapter 3, which describe how God will send a messenger to prepare his way as a refiner's fire and a fuller's soap. The imagery of both fire and lye soap reveals aggressive agents that test and cleanse. Even though our Lord doesn't change, he is determined to remake us into all we were created to be.

The very fact that God doesn't change should give us the courage to believe that we can! He is consistently good and faithful.

When my sons were young, they would naturally try to push their limits and mine. It wasn't always that they wanted their own way. At times they wanted to know their real boundaries. Did I really mean what I said? How many times would I say, "If you throw that ball again in the house, you will lose it" before it was actually removed? Would there be follow-through or vain threats?

When I was inconsistent, there was confusion for everyone involved. If I said one thing when I was happy and another when I was tired, there was no way of knowing what I might say if I was caught in another type of mood. If I said one thing to them when I was with other people and another in private, they weren't sure where I was going with things. Until I was consistent, they were hesitant or even disobedient.

> The very fact that God doesn't change should give us the courage to believe that we can!

Recently, I was on a phone call with someone we have invited into our world to help us make more room for others in our organization. He asked me why I lacked confidence in one area of our organization when I was completely confident in another. We realized it came down to a lack of clarity. What was my role? I wasn't sure where I had authority and where I didn't. When you don't know what to expect, you don't know how to act.

We were made for clarity. God knows this. God is constant and consistent in his nature. God is good. God does good. God gives us what is good. There is no reason for us to allow doubt to shadow our thinking.

> Every good gift and every perfect gift is from above, coming down from the Father of lights, with whom there is no variation or shadow due to change. (James 1:17)

The Message paraphrases the second half of James 1:17 as "there is nothing deceitful in God, nothing two-faced, nothing fickle." Our Father is not trying to trick us or catch us off guard by saying one thing while actually meaning another. He will not say one thing to our faces and something different behind our backs. Our God is reliable and speaks openly a consistent message to all.

Another Scripture passage that expresses his unfailing consistency is Numbers 23:19:

> God is not man, that he should lie, or a son of man, that he should change his mind. Has he said, and will he not do it? Or has he spoken, and will he not fulfill it?

God does not lie. He does not change his mind. He will do what he said he would. What he speaks will be fully realized. Something may look different or arrive later than we expected, but it will happen.

God is our adamant, immovable mountain, the constant Rock that is higher so that we can lift our eyes, knowing he is always there. Because he is constant, his Word and his ways are consistent with each other. He cannot say one thing and then act in another manner. He is unified in all his expressions.

The *letter* of what was said in the Old Testament may look different in its application in the New Testament but never the *spirit* of it. Under the Abrahamic covenant, circumcision was required for every male, but as the gospel spread to the Gentiles, it was no longer a requirement. Paul explains it this way:

> For circumcision indeed is of value if you obey the law, but if you break the law, your circumcision becomes uncircumcision. So, if a man who is uncircumcised keeps the precepts of the law, will not his uncircumcision be regarded as circumcision? Then he who is physically uncircumcised but keeps the law will condemn you who have the written code and circumcision but break the law. For no one is a Jew who is merely one outwardly, nor is circumcision outward and physical. But a Jew is one inwardly, and *circumcision is a matter of the heart, by the Spirit, not by the letter.* His praise is not from man but from God. (Rom. 2:25–29)

What good is an outward sign if it is not accompanied by an inward transformation? And yet true inward transformation doesn't require an outward application of the law. Ultimately, it was always a circumcised heart God was after. This is an intimate issue that weaves the heart of the Father and the spirit of the law, which produces obedience. The spirit of a law will always supersede the fleshly requirement. The Spirit empowers us in ways the law never could. God didn't change his mind . . . he changed our hearts. Read what he said to Moses:

> But I lavish unfailing love for a thousand generations on those who love me and obey my commands. (Deut. 5:10 NLT)

And again:

> Oh, that they would always have hearts like this, that they might fear me and obey all my commands! If they did, they and their descendants would prosper forever. (Deut. 5:29 NLT)

Throughout the testament of mankind, the winning combination has always been love and obedience. Love empowers us to obey. God longed to lavish us with unfailing love, not overwhelm us with a list of impossible laws. If God could have reached in and changed our hearts long ago at the foot of Mount Sinai, he would have. But instead, he sent Jesus to show us his heart. Once his love for us was revealed, the only laws that were necessary were the laws of love. Again we read:

He sent Jesus to show us his heart.

> Jesus answered, "The most important is, 'Hear, O Israel: The Lord our God, the Lord is one. And you shall love the Lord your God with all your heart and with all your soul and with all your mind and with all your strength.' The second is this: 'You shall love your neighbor as yourself.' There is no other commandment greater than these." (Mark 12:29–31)

The Ten Commandments of the Old Testament had evolved into a plethora of moral laws, ceremonial laws, and civil laws, and yet Jesus said, "On these two commandments depend all the Law and the Prophets" (Matt. 22:40).

I Am

The next part of the sentence I unpacked was the phrase "I am," which is actually a complete sentence on its own. And it is one that answers so many of the questions we humans raise.

"God, are you there?"

He replies, "I am."

"Will you take care of this?"

Again he assures us, "I am."

He is simultaneously in our past, present, and future as the "I Am."

He was faithful because he is faithful. He will be faithful because he has been faithful. Because he is . . . I am.

As I wrote *Without Rival*, I was overwhelmed by the concept of the God Most High, the great I Am. In an age when so many are obsessed with discovering who they are, it should be a relief to all of us to learn that we discover our identity in the One who was, and is, and is to come. Our identity is like so much treasure hidden deep within him. We discover who we are in the revelation of whose we are.

I am a child of the I Am.

You are a child of the I Am.

God introduced himself to Moses as "I AM WHO I AM" (Exod. 3:14), which is one way of saying, "I am the total embodiment of all that I am with nothing partial and nothing missing."

The King James version reads, "I Am That I Am" (Exod. 3:14). God exists because he exists. I exist because he exists. Because he exists, he is not unaware. God appeared to Moses because he had heard the cry of a generation enslaved in the cruel bondage of Egypt. Because he was aware, he got involved.

> I have observed you and what has been done to you in Egypt, and I promise that I will bring you up out of the affliction of Egypt. (Exod. 3:16–17)

As I read and think about our I Am God, I see three things: God sees, God knows, God responds. These three points say, "I am aware." I don't know where you are, but at this very moment, the I Am sees you, knows what has been done, and promises to deliver you from both your affliction and your bondage.

He is all. He is the beginning and the end and yet is without beginning or end. He encompasses every letter from alpha to omega and yet cannot be described by any multitude of words the assembling of letters could create. He is the I Am. God is the reason for reason.

All creation proceeds from the Creator. Because he is . . . I am. Because he is . . . you are. Our Creator is our origin and the ultimate author of our identity. This means no one could ever steal an identity hidden in him. In Christ, our Adamant, we are his, not by right of our natural birth but by the gracious gift and right of our rebirth.

The next piece of the sentence that stood out to me was "the Lord."

This terminology wraps the I Am in supremacy, such as in "the Lord, the Most High" (Ps. 7:17). It is also the term used in association with Yahweh, a name so holy that Jews consider it too sacred to be spoken. This holy and high name is his identity wrapped in his compassion and mercy.

I am thankful that the Lord of all that is high and holy is both compassionate and merciful. What if the One of ultimate authority was a callous, ruthless dictator instead? The truth is, because he is the Lord of all, he is worthy of my all. Because he is merciful and compassionate, he understands that for each of us life is a journey.

> In him, we do not become less ourselves; rather, we are freed to become more of who he created us to be.

When we surrender to all that he is (Lord), our lives are enlarged by his domain. In him, we do not become less ourselves; rather, we are freed to become more of who he created us to be. It is hard for us to imagine the use of the word *lord* outside the realms of our experience with human hierarchy. We have known earthly lords who leveraged their positions of power and authority for their own benefit. Throughout human history, renegade lords have used those under their domain. Jesus warned his disciples about this dynamic in Matthew 20:25–28:

> But Jesus called them to him and said, "You know that the rulers of the Gentiles lord it over them, and their great ones exercise authority over them. It shall not be so among you. But whoever would be great among you must be your servant, and whoever would be first among you must be your slave, even as the Son of Man came not to be served but to serve, and to give his life as a ransom for many."

The lordship of Jesus lifts us rather than holds us down. Every aspect of the life of Jesus served and ransomed. Our Lord was stripped so that we could be covered. Jesus was compromised so that we could receive what was promised. Our Lord was betrayed so that we could be protected. Jesus was raised from death unto life so that we too could be raised.

The next portion of the phrase I looked at was "thy God." I am not quite sure why I heard "thy God" in my spirit rather than "your God." Perhaps it is from reciting the "Our Father" innumerable times over the course of my life. Or it might be a nod to the timelessness of this declaration.

The use of the word *God* here denotes *Elohim*, the Creator, the Judge, and the Warrior. The truth is, he didn't become God when I acknowledged him as such. He was always my Creator God. He didn't need my acknowledgment to know me. He knew me before and knows me now far better than I know myself. He wove me in secret and woos me in the secret place. As my Judge, he has acquitted my sin and removed my iniquities. Psalm 103:10–12 says:

> He does not deal with us according to our sins,
>   nor repay us according to our iniquities.
> For as high as the heavens are above the earth,
>   so great is *his steadfast love toward those who*
>   *fear him*;
> as far as the east is from the west,
>   so far does he remove our transgressions from us.

God's love is unfathomable and immovable, impenetrable and impervious. Which leads us directly back into the last phrase I heard: "I change not."

Just as God is adamant in love, he is adamant in mercy. He swears by his unchanging nature rather than our changeable one. In Psalm 103:17, we read how his love is promised to those who fear him. God is not looking for perfection, because outside of Christ, our adamant Cornerstone, there are no sinless people! But he *is* looking for those who fear him. Why? What does it mean to fear God in our day of familiarity and irreverence?

One way to fear the Lord is to depart from evil. In Proverbs 3:7, we read, "Be not wise in your own eyes; fear the LORD, and turn away from evil." The Passion Translation says it this way: "For wisdom comes when you adore him with undivided devotion and avoid everything that's wrong."

When we combine the meanings found in these two interpretations of the same verse, we conclude that as we look to him in awe and cultivate wonder, we turn from everything that is evil and wrong. The wonder of the unchanging one changes us.

Because he loves, he cares. Because he cares, he is constant.

Dear heavenly Father,
You are faithful and loving even when I am fearful and
faithless. I pray that in an ever-changing world, I will
know you as my constant. Change me to reflect your
steadfast nature and enduring love. In a world of in-
consistency, I want to be consistent.

4

ADAMANT IN LOVE

The supreme happiness of life is the conviction
that we are loved; loved for ourselves, or rather
in spite of ourselves.

Victor Hugo

It was more than thirty-five years ago that John gave me my diamond engagement ring. He wanted to make it official that I was his and he was mine. (Even though he had been telling everyone I was his long before that!) To buy the ring, John ate only potatoes and saved like a miser for months. On June 6, 1982, my twenty-second birthday, as we sat by a fountain in Dallas, John presented me with a velvet box. My hands and heart trembled as I opened it. Within the black cube I discovered a single tear-shaped diamond set high on a simple band of gold. It was magnificent. As far as I was concerned, there had never been a more beautiful diamond. Tears filled my eyes as I said yes and promptly slipped the ring on my finger.

I remember it was too big, but there was no way I was taking it off! That night I slept with a smile on my face and a ring on my finger. We were engaged!

I woke up the next morning, and my engagement ring was the first thing I looked at. The diamond that sparkled in the morning sunshine and cast flecks of rainbows on my dreary apartment wall assured me that the night before had not been a dream. In the year leading up to our engagement, there had been some drama between John and me. After a few breakups early on in our relationship, it was good to know we were moving forward with a commitment to love each other. When John and I went to church that morning, so many people congratulated us. I was more than happy to fan my hand and show my ring, but what I was really flaunting was our love.

I'm pretty sure that even though I'm right-handed, my left hand began to take the leading role whenever I was with someone. We lived in Dallas, which meant there would always be larger diamonds with more flash than mine, but those diamonds weren't my diamond. My diamond told the story of our adamant commitment to love each other. We were vowing to have and to hold each other in good times and in bad, in lean years and in years of plenty, in strength and in weakness, until death separated us. It said a new story of love had begun. And for all of us, God has done the same.

God is love.

Love is our Father's nature. He doesn't love us because he has to; he loves because he cannot *not* love us. God didn't tolerate us in the Old Testament and decide to love us in the New. He didn't decide to love us because Jesus told him to. His love for us was what set our rescue in motion. He gave his Son to express his love for us. His love cannot be conquered by rejection and self-loathing. We could never convince him to stop loving us, for long ago, before we had any say in the matter, he set his love over us as a banner and welcomed us at his table.

God doesn't have love *for* us. God *is* love for us. God's love for us is adamant, invincible, steadfast, and stronger than death.

> Who is like you, O LORD, among the gods? Who is like you, majestic in holiness, awesome in glorious deeds, doing wonders? You stretched out your right hand; the earth swallowed them. You have led in your *steadfast love* the people whom you have redeemed; you have guided them by your strength to your holy abode. (Exod. 15:11–13)

God leads with love.

His love is our true north, the one constant by which we can navigate life. Without the assurance of this love, it is easy for us to lose our way and wander off course. Ultimately, it is his love that leads us home.

The psalm of Moses in Exodus 15 was written after God had magnificently rescued his people after hundreds of years of Egyptian oppression. We know

His love *for* us is not dependent *on* us.

the story, but what I want to highlight here is the adjective attached to God's love: *steadfast*. It is another assurance that his love for us does not waver. The flame of his love does not flicker in the wind of our waywardness. His love remains when we are irresponsible, unresponsive, and rebellious. He cannot bless these actions, but even in the midst of them, his kindness leads us to repentance and his love does not falter.

His love *for* us is not dependent *on* us. His affection toward us does not vary according to our behavior. He always has loved us. He always will love us. We cannot earn what we never deserved any more than we can pay for what has been given.

> "For the mountains may depart and the hills be removed, but my *steadfast love shall not depart from you*, and my covenant of peace shall not be removed," says the LORD, who has compassion on you. (Isa. 54:10)

His love will not leave us. People may come and go, but his constant, adamant love will remain. Because his love is immovable, we have been wrapped in a covenant of peace. Jesus, our adamant Cornerstone, is the Prince of Peace. From his realm of highest power, he whispers peace to every storm in our bodies and to every tempest that assaults our minds. His compassion for us knows no bounds. We can be at peace because there is no denying his love for us. To deny his love for us, God would have to deny his love for his Son.

Because of his adamant love for us, we were redeemed in Christ, our Adamant. You may ask, "How can I be sure this is true?" His love for us can be seen: "But God shows his love for us in that while we were still sinners, Christ died for us" (Rom. 5:8).

Love Is a Choice

Diamonds capture more than the potential of married love; they express attributes of love itself. Like diamonds, love is conceived in wombs of fire and pressure. There can be seasons, years, or even decades when love is buried deep under the surface like a hidden spring. You know it is there. It was planted years ago deep within the soil of your life, yet you cannot see its beauty or feel its fire . . . all you sense is its subterranean whisper.

Love in its truest form is not a feeling. It is a choice. Love is why an exhausted mother rouses herself from sleep to respond to the frightened cry of a child. Love is why a father works long hours to provide for his children. (And yes, love means there are times when these roles are reversed.) The point is that love gives even when it is not returned.

Once Love has chosen, he does not change his mind.

We love because Love chose us. You love because God chose you (1 John 4:19). And our Father loves even when we don't.

First Love

God is and will always be our first love. He loved us first, and this first love isn't immature; it is adamant. He does not love us in the hope we will be like someone else. There was never another that he compares you to . . . it was always you. It was always the collective us he loved. Though we first loved others, he first loved us. But eventually, we each discover the adamancy of our first love, this steadfast, invincible love.

Perhaps there are areas that you feel your actions have changed the way God feels about you? Maybe there are places and patterns in which you have developed a habit of disobedience or inconsistency?

I understand. I ran away from his love for far too many years. I didn't understand what his love looked like. I argued that if he truly loved me he would give me what I wanted. I imagined that the love of one of his sons would make me happy here and now. To be frank, I had horrible taste in men.

I chose the ones who were hard to please who turned into the ones who were hard to keep. God looked beyond my wants and answered my greatest need. His love.

He gave me a greater love than those that could be won or lost.

I still remember that crystalline moment when his love came into focus. I saw it before me. I recognized its rays as though peering through so many facets of a single diamond, each plane pointing to that fraction of time when I was born again and betrothed to my Bridegroom, Jesus Christ.

> **God's love for you is more adamant than a diamond.**

God's love for you is more adamant than a diamond. It will not vaporize in a vacuum of intense light. His engagement to you went deeper than a ring. He would never trust a promise so precious to an item that could be misplaced or stolen. His claim was hidden away and treasured as a seal upon his favorite part of you . . . your heart.

These verses in Song of Songs eavesdrop on an intimate conversation that declares unending bonds of passion between lovers:

> Set me as a seal upon your heart,
>   as a seal upon your arm,
> for love is strong as death,
>   jealousy is fierce as the grave.
> Its flashes are flashes of fire,
>   the very flame of the LORD.
> Many waters cannot quench love,
>   neither can floods drown it.
> If a man offered for love all the wealth of his house,
>   he would be utterly despised. (8:6–7)

Does this love make you uncomfortable? Maybe it is difficult for you to imagine yourself worthy of someone loving you with this much intensity. Maybe you doubt your capacity to return such love. These words were not penned to make you doubt the love you have experienced or even to cause you to question your capacity to love. This intimate glimpse is given to reveal the passionate type of love you were created for.

It is impossible to measure God's love for us by our human experiences. There is no reference point in this fallen span of time. The lucky in love have known sparks that led to gentle warmth. Others have known sparks that eventually betrayed them when over the years their fires were neglected and the coals of human love turned to ashes.

Rare is the human love that can be described as a sustained fire. And yet we long for it. If we are honest, we will acknowledge the whisper of our hearts and admit that we want to feel this level of intensity with an intimate other.

Sometimes I am almost embarrassed by the passion captured in the Song of Songs. Then I remember that my role is simply to respond, not to reason. As I lay aside my questions and acknowledge and then receive God's jealous, strong, fierce love, the fire of my love for God is fanned.

This passage is ultimately a description of Christ and his bride. In this shadowed realm of earth, we know all things only in parts and pieces. In the eternal realm, when we will know as we are known, love will be unveiled in all its fiery splendor.

The fire of God's love for us cannot be quenched. The floods of life may threaten, but they cannot drown the love God has for us.

God's love is not for sale. There is nothing that we call wealth that he'd ever exchange for us.

And even though this passage refers to God's love for the bride of Christ, which is the church collective, this love is as protective and personal as a mother's and as intimate as a lover's. Our Father could not love well the whole if he did not first love well the parts.

Sealed

We could never make ourselves worthy of such an all-consuming love, so God has done the work for us.

> And it is God who establishes us with you in Christ, and has anointed us, and who has also put his seal on us and given us his Spirit in our hearts as a guarantee. (2 Cor. 1:21–22)

I cannot establish myself. You cannot establish yourself. A church membership will not establish us in unity. His Spirit makes us one.

Listen to how these verses read in the Passion Translation:

> Now, it is God himself who has anointed us. And he is constantly strengthening both you and us in union with Christ. He knows we are his since he stamped his seal of love over our hearts and has given us the Holy Spirit like an engagement ring is given to a bride—a down payment for blessings to come!

Do you see this? Even if you didn't know it, you are definitely engaged!

Our modern-day seals are flimsy wrappers found on vitamins or food products. These wrappers confirm the package has not yet been opened, while at the same time they are made to open easily. This type of seal is different from the seal described in 2 Corinthians. This seal comes from the Greek word *sphragizo*, which describes a sevenfold seal that includes the following:

1. seal of security (we are tightly kept in God's love)
2. seal of authentication (we are marked as God's very own)
3. seal of genuineness
4. seal of ownership
5. seal of approval
6. seal of righteousness
7. seal of promise[1]

> They warn the forces of darkness that we are *not* to be tampered with.

These seals are more than tamper evident. They warn the forces of darkness that we are *not* to be tampered with. Not one of these seals can be broken by us because they are tied to Christ's obedience, not our own. Not only are these seals a "hands off" message, but each layer is a divine affirmation of God's betrothal. We cannot reach within ourselves and place these seals upon our hearts. Love reached in and sealed us until the day love will reveal us.

Love's Eternal Gifts

You and I were born of the Spirit, sealed with the Spirit, indwelt by the Spirit, baptized in the Spirit, made one in the Spirit, given gifts by the Spirit, and commissioned into ministry by the Spirit. Everything we need was provided by our God, who loves us without end.

This is the very reason Ephesians assures each of us of the following:

> I'm writing this letter to all the devoted believers who have been made holy by being one with Jesus, the Anointed One. May God himself, the heavenly Father of our Lord Jesus Christ, release grace over you and impart total well-being into your lives. (1:2 TPT)

Do you see our heavenly Father's intimate involvement in this process? We say yes to a life of devoted belief by pledging our hearts. In turn, God graces us to receive the fullness of his divine impartation into our lives. Ephesians goes on to say:

> Everything heaven contains has already been lavished upon us as a love gift from our wonderful heavenly Father, the Father of our Lord Jesus—all because he sees us wrapped into Christ. This is why we celebrate him with all our hearts! (1:3 TPT)

We celebrate *now* in the hope of *then*. It is in the eternal realm that true life begins. It is there that all the contents of heaven await his bride as a perpetual wedding gift. In case you fear this version is overstating the gifts of love that await you, read this verse in the English Standard Version:

> Blessed be the God and Father of our Lord Jesus Christ, who has blessed us in Christ with *every spiritual blessing in the heavenly places.*

No blessing heaven has to offer has been left out or withheld. The extravagant provision for his bride is in step with the extravagance of his love for her. And you are part of the package.

As his bride, you and I were wrapped into Christ, the Anointed One. Just as what he *did* covers what we have *done*, his death and resurrection empower what we will *do* in him. His submitted obedience eliminated the debt and penalty of our disobedience just as it enabled us to be obedient. If you are devoted to this belief, then this letter of Paul was written to you and of you.

As believers in Christ, we who are the many are made one in the indestructible cornerstone of the Holy One. Not only are we wrapped into Christ, but our lives are also graced with an impartation of well-being.

In so many ways and on so many fronts, grace is the proverbial ribbon that adorns this package of promise. God sealed us within his heart and sealed our hearts within the adamant cornerstone of his love.

Lovely one, hear me. You do not inhabit a hollowed-out hole in Christ, chiseled out sparingly to make room for you. In Christ, the adamant Cornerstone, you have access to the whole. You are not an intruder. You are not a guest . . . you are family. Actually, family isn't intimate enough. We are one within Jesus even as he is one with the Father. We are part of the all in all.

Both provision and a place have been prepared for us. This abundance includes all the fruit of the Spirit, our gifting in the Spirit, and peace, righteousness, and joy. Let's keep our hearts and treasure in the right place. Let's set them on things above, where they will not be corrupted or stolen from us.

Once we possess the knowledge of this love, why would any of us even think of eyeing the suitors of this earthly realm? The prince of the powers of the air has no love for us.

He hates us . . . adamantly.

Any promise the dark prince makes is a lie. Any power he grants is attached to this frail and fallen realm, which is destined to crumble. Any gift or talent Satan bestows reveals itself as a theft. He cannot give; he can only take. He cannot help but pervert all he touches.

> The prince of the powers of the air has no love for us.

But we are no longer subjects of his realm, and we know that every good and true gift comes from our Father. We also know that nothing can separate us from the love of Christ.

Safe in Christ's Love

Who shall separate us from the love of Christ? Shall tribulation, or distress, or persecution, or famine, or nakedness, or danger, or sword? As it is written, "For your sake we are being killed all the day long; we are regarded as sheep to be slaughtered." No, in all these things we are more than conquerors through him who loved us. For I am sure that neither death nor life, nor angels nor rulers, nor things present nor things to come, nor powers, nor height nor depth, nor anything else in all creation, will be able to separate us from the love of God in Christ Jesus our Lord. (Rom. 8:35–39)

Nothing can separate us from the adamant love of Christ. There is no who, there is no what. His love cannot be taken, for we have been placed in Christ. The cruelty of conflict and the dangers of war can never make him side against us. There is no disaster large enough to unseat the love of our Prince of Peace. His love is more certain than death and more real than life. His love for us supersedes the domains of both the angelic and the demonic realms. There is nothing that has been, is, or will be in the entire span of creation that will ever have the capacity to divorce us from the love of God in Christ Jesus our Lord. His love for us is as adamant as his love for Jesus. God would have to reject his Son to reject us.

Loved before Time

> And he chose us to be his very own, joining us to himself even before he laid the foundation of the universe! Because of his great love, he ordained us as one with Christ from the beginning, so that we would be seen as holy in his eyes with an unstained innocence. (Eph. 1:4 TPT)

I'm always so excited to show people my children, my daughter-in-law, and my grandchildren. When I read these words, I get the sense that God is even more excited about you than I am about my family. He looks at you and proudly declares, "This one is mine!" He betrothed you to himself and then created a universe for you to live in with him forever.

You were not chosen the day you turned to Christ—that is the day you chose. No, my friend, you were chosen in Christ long before the fountains of the deep were formed. You were formed in Christ so that through the power of transformation he might be formed in you. You came alive to this truth the day you were born again. Through the death of God's Son, love not only rescued you but also restored you to his initial hope.

Not only are you engaged, but you were also foreordained or designed to be one with Christ. No one can keep this kind of love quiet!

In the adamancy of his love, God wrapped us in the unstained innocence of Christ long before Adam and Eve even had the chance to strip themselves of light and truth and robe themselves in the serpent's shrouds of sin and death.

Knowing myself, I would have suggested that God wrap me up in black garments rather than garments of radiant white. The quote by Coco Chanel describes my wardrobe choices perfectly: "When I find a color darker than black, I'll wear it. But until then, I'm wearing black!"

In black, there is no need to worry about stains. They may be there, but no one can see them. It is the very reason I travel in predominantly black clothing. Dressed in black, I can move confidently through airports weekend after weekend. In black tops, I can sweat unseen, wield permanent Sharpie markers without fear, and hug weeping women without any concern of a makeup transfer. Keeping black, black . . . is easy. Keeping white, white . . . is not so easy.

Not long ago, I forgot why I don't travel in white. It had been a long winter in Colorado, so when spring finally came, I donned white jeans for my weekend away. Feeling fresh, I trotted out to the car. My gracious host handed me my now-favorite drink . . . a short, three-shot, coconut milk flat white with cinnamon. In joyous anticipation, I pulled out the stirrer that acts like a stopper, and presto, I had spots. The rest of the drink was consumed over the center console of the rental car. As soon as I arrived at the church, we attacked the coffee stain with a Tide bleach pen. As I watched the toxic chemicals leach through my jeans into my upper thigh, my white jeans turned blue. Hoping this chemical reaction meant the stain was gone, I doused my upper thigh with copious amounts of water. The two-inch splatter of coffee had now spread to a circle eight inches wide that just so happened to cover the broadest section of my upper thigh. The stain appeared to be gone, but you can never be certain until your jeans are dry. Meanwhile, the portion of my jeans that covered my upper thigh was transparent. Thus dressed, I took the stage.

God knows we cannot maintain a spotless life, so in Christ it is washed for us. In Christ, there are no hidden stains; in Christ, there are no bleach pens; in Christ, there are no see-through pants that expose fluffy thighs. In Christ, there is strength and radiance.

> For it was *always* in his perfect plan to adopt us as his delight-ful children, so that his tremendous grace that cascades over us would bring him glory—for the same love he has for his Beloved One, Jesus, he has for us! (Eph. 1:5–6 TPT)

Have you ever been invited as an afterthought? I certainly have! Or maybe you got yourself invited to something because the host discovered that you knew you weren't included. Again, me too! That is not what is happening here. You are not an add-on, an afterthought, or someone who was included at the last minute. You have *always* been welcome!

> In Christ, there is strength and radiance.

Our adoption into God's family was planned from the very beginning. He didn't bring us near because he felt sorry for us or because no one else wanted us. He delights in us because in Christ he sees what we will be rather than what we have been.

I love the word imagery here . . . cascades. I can't help but picture a waterfall. Have you ever stood under one? The water tumbles over you with unrestrained force and in amounts without measure. If the source of the water is abundant and the distance the water falls is far, there will be a mist. The very mist of God's tremendous grace anoints those who draw near through his love. And in case we might be tempted to imagine this cataract as a trickle, the next verse cancels all such thoughts:

> Since we are now joined to Christ, we have been given the treasures of salvation by his blood—the total cancellation of our sins—all because of the cascading riches of his grace. (Eph. 1:7 TPT)

Cascading grace. Outside of Christ, I wouldn't deserve a drop of grace and mercy. I would deserve only the full weight and stain of far more sins than I could even remember to confess. That is who I am outside of him.

And yet . . .

His love for us is as intimate as the breath we draw and as far-reaching as the wind that wraps the globe.

His love for us is exclusive and unique.

His love for us is all-inclusive. There is no part of us that escapes his love. He loves us without exception.

Love is our connection with the eternal realm of God. When I call God's love adamant, I do so to assure you that it is not only unshakable but also insistent. God's love chases us down and persistently demands our notice. The love of God remains consistent in its posture of pursuit. He will not be dissuaded from his position. He is for us. No matter how destructive our behavior, his love for us is indestructible. We can war against God's love, but in the end, it is invincible.

Love Won

Currently, there are many hashtags #lovewins.

Love cannot *help* but win because God is love. Because this eternal victory has already taken place, it is more correct to say #lovewon. Love wins implies a present or future triumph. You may wonder why I feel the tense matters. When I study what is going on around the globe, it would appear the proper hashtag is #hatewins. I am hard-pressed to see more than fleeting glimpses of love. But ultimately, hate cannot win because hate is not eternal . . . love is. "Love wins" implies fluidity, when actually the victory of love was fixed in our favor before the beginning of time. "Love won" declares a victory that took place long before we existed and therefore utterly without our involvement. "Love won" cannot be canceled by our actions. It need only be affirmed by our worship.

Love won us before we loved.

The words of "Reckless Love" captures the actions of God's adamant love:

> Before I spoke a word
> You were singing over me
> You have been so, so
> Good to me
> Before I took a breath
> You breathed Your life in me
> You have been so, so
> Kind to me

79

Oh, the overwhelming, never-ending, reckless love of
  God
Oh, it chases me down, fights 'til I'm found, leaves
  the ninety-nine
I couldn't earn it
I don't deserve it
Still You give yourself away
Oh, the overwhelming, never-ending, reckless love of
  God

When I was your foe, still Your love fought for me
You have been so, so
Good to me
When I felt no worth
You paid it all for me
You have been so, so
Kind to me

There's no shadow You won't light up
Mountain You won't climb up
Coming after me
There's no wall You won't kick down
No lie You won't tear down
Coming after me[2]

Dear heavenly Father,
Your love is extravagant. Thank you for sealing me in
your love, for choosing to love me, for planning for my
life from the very first breath. Today let me choose to
love as you have loved me. Thank you for loving me
enough to adamantly remove every obstacle between us.
Tear down every wall and lie that yet stands between
us. Amen.

5

ADAMANT THAT WE LOVE

Love is the only force capable of transforming an
enemy into a friend.

Martin Luther King Jr.

I want to share a story with you that captures both the
intimate love and the constant care of our Father God.
Recently, I went to Iraq. I was invited to speak at an
event in Dubai and decided it would be the perfect opportunity to visit a ministry called Preemptive Love.

My first day there I shadowed Jessica and Jeremy Courtney
as they visited clusters of Yazidi refugees they were helping
to rebuild their lives after ISIS had decimated and displaced
them. Because I do not speak Arabic or any of the Kurd-
ish dialects, all I could do was watch and listen as Jessica
interacted with the women and families she had set up with
soap-making businesses.

I still remember the reaction of these precious people. They lit up when they saw Jessica. On so many levels, she represented hope; she was someone who believed in them. They greeted her warmly and offered whatever food or drink they had to share. Their homes were makeshift tents, concrete block rooms, containers, and abandoned truck trailers. On the last stop of the night, we gathered with fourteen people who had taken shelter in a semi trailer. The little children ran out to greet Jessica and surrounded her, practicing phrases of English to impress her.

I couldn't help but notice the one small girl who hung back, her face averted. When Jessica sat down, the little girls clustered around her as she held a conversation with the refugee women and a few men. But the one girl sat apart. I learned that ISIS had killed her father, and her mother was away. I felt drawn to her. I asked Jessica for her story and learned that she had lost an eye to a malignant tumor. My heart quickened. I asked Jessica if she'd call the girl over and translate for me. I didn't guess her to be more than seven years old. She came haltingly and hesitantly, following the words and encouragement of those who were present.

I drew her onto my lap, aware of how awkward and frightening it was to be singled out by a complete stranger.

But Sarah and I had more in common than she knew.

I told Sarah how I had lost my eye to a tumor when I was five. She turned and looked intently at my face, searching to see if what I said was true. Then she scanned the faces of those in the trailer. I wondered if she was saying, "I found someone who understands."

I had my iPad in my purse. I shared family pictures with Sarah as I whispered in her ear words Jessica was kind enough to translate.

"Sarah, you can dream. Sarah, you can have a family. Sarah, you can do anything God puts in your heart."

I wanted her to know that the loss of an eye did not equate to the loss of a life.

After all she'd been through, perhaps the loss of an eye was a small thing. Yet I didn't want it to limit and define her. Jessica had not known that I too had lost an eye. She explained how difficult it was to keep Sarah's eye clean. The artificial eye was filmed over with dust. I gently tried to close her eyelid. It was not possible. This artificial eye was made for an adult and far too large to allow for her eyelid to close. Jessica explained that they had gone to a lot of trouble to secure this eye for her. It was the best they could find in Iraq.

I held Sarah's hand as we walked back to the car.

We were both silent.

That night as I lay sleepless in the basement of the Courtneys' home, my thoughts turned to her. I'd never know the pain of losing a father to such a violent, senseless death or what it was like to leave behind everything I'd ever known. I couldn't do anything about what had been done, but maybe something could be done about her eye.

A few months passed, and I learned that Jessica was in the States. I reached out and discovered we'd actually be in California together at the same event. My ocularist in Colorado Springs, Mitchell Mayo, just happened to have worked with Yazidi children and knew the nuances of their eye color. He was more than happy to help and provided me with a number of child-sized artificial eyes for Sarah.

Jessica and I connected in California, where I recorded a greeting for Sarah that Jessica would later interpret.

That afternoon Jessica was on a panel. I listened and wept as she shared how my visit had touched Sarah. By paying attention to this forlorn little girl, I had elevated her to princess status.

Isn't this just like our Lord? He singles out the ones who don't want to be seen and gives the hopeless permission to dream.

Jessica returned to Iraq with eyes for Sarah. I will let Jessica's words from Instagram tell the story of what this gift of an eye did in Sarah's life:

> Sarah watched as Lisa told her she was remembered, beautiful, that she could do anything and everything she wants, and how much God loves her! As I translated the message to her, tears welled and I wondered how many times she had been called out as beautiful, cherished, remembered, and known.

Next Jessica posted the picture of Sarah's mother changing out the old eye for her new one. Her extended family crowded around, waiting to see what it would look like. Her uncle spoke of the love and care they share with one another. Her aunt couldn't contain her excitement about the big difference this little detail had made. The last set of pictures captured the entire story: Sarah with the life-threatening tumor, Sarah with the plastic eye she was able to get in Iraq, Sarah with her new eye, and Sarah surrounded by family and friends. Here is Jessica's dialogue describing the change:

> I wish you could all see the difference in this little girl, the way she holds her head up proudly and isn't shy to jump into a picture the way she was before. Or how she was leading the conversation yesterday when we joined them for lunch,

and how I didn't even recognize her because her demeanor is totally different. Love changes everything, this one little girl and entire communities.

God's goodness is constant, and his love endures forever. I am humbled that God would allow me to visit Iraq if only to meet a little girl who lost her eye to the same type of tumor I did so that she would know his love.

Love's Pattern

To say that my mother and I had relational challenges is an understatement of grand proportions. As far back as I can remember, there was an undercurrent of tension between us. Over the last ten years, whenever I called her, the conversation would quickly escalate to a misunderstanding of some sort. And yet even now I am hard-pressed to remember the harsh words that passed between us.

What I remember are the words I didn't say.

I wish I'd been more intentional to show and tell her I loved her. When it came to expressing love, my mother and I spoke languages as different as Italian and English. Sadly, I refused to become bilingual until much too late. Yes, in the last month of her life I said all the things I wished I had. I told her I loved her. I asked her to forgive me for any and every grievance, large or small. I lay across her hospital bed and held her frail frame, careful not to upset the tubes and wires that tethered her to the metal frame. She leaned close and

> What I remember are the words I didn't say.

whispered a reprieve. That's when the levee broke. We both cried, overwhelmed by the knowledge that we had so little time to live out this love this side of eternity. In less than a month, she was gone.

The promise of eternity has softened the blow of this reality. But even so, regret can be a hard taskmaster. In the past, I've responded to its accusations and remorse by making excuses or casting blame. But over the years, I've adopted a different and at times more difficult approach: I own my mistakes. At first this proved a far more painful option because it pushes the wound to the forefront. Even so, brave one . . . do it. I promise it will save you so much unnecessary hurt in the long run.

The truth is I should have loved my mother better sooner. I was in the stronger position to love her well, and I didn't. While I can't change the past, I am left with clear choices going forward. I can feel bad and the sadness will stay with me, or I can flip my mistakes into lessons for others. You see, once you own a mistake, it no longer owns you. Learn from me. You will never regret kind words, warmth, or acts of generosity—but you will regret the love you never gave.

> Once you own a mistake, it no longer owns you.

Love well, beautiful friends, and you will live well. Love is our agent of transformation. Our heavenly Father, who is adamant in his love for us, is likewise adamant that we love one another. There are so many people we now call enemies who are actually just hurting people who are desperate to be loved. As followers of Christ, we do not have the option of not loving them. Loving one another was a command rather than a suggestion: "This is my commandment, that you love one another as I have loved you" (John 15:12).

Those five words are the challenge: "as I have loved you."

Jesus is our pattern.

I made the mistake of loving my mother in response to the pattern of how she loved me. For most of my life, my mother and I did the awkward dance of two steps forward followed by two steps back with neither of us getting anywhere. A year before she died, she told me that the tension between us was not my fault. She explained that she had simply never bonded with me. Her words hurt, even though I believe she meant them to help. I think it was her hope that the admission would release me.

Now I know that this lack of a maternal bond didn't matter. We were bonded in Christ.

How different it all would have been if I had loved as Jesus loves me.

So what does it mean to follow a pattern? To answer, I am going to reach back into junior high. It was then that we were required to take home economics, which included a brief foray into sewing. The patterns we used were made out of light-brown tissue paper traced with solid and dotted lines for our scissors and pins to follow. The idea was to fit the pattern to the person before cutting out the fabric.

Later on, when I made things on my own, I read the instructions and studied the patterns looking for shortcuts. I wanted to finish fast, so I skipped finishing the seams. And all of you smarter people know what happened. The clothes would look good for a little while, but sooner rather than later they would unravel and holes would appear. In love and in sewing, there are no shortcuts . . . we are instructed to follow the pattern.

When it comes to loving others, too many of us haven't finished our seams because we didn't want to take the time that was required to prepare the fabric of our relationships. We closed the gaps and made them look finished on the outside, but the inside was a mess of loose thread and tense fabric. Looking for shortcuts, we settled for excuses, such as, "I can't love well—I didn't grow up in a Christian household."

Love how Jesus loves you. This may seem a bit abstract at times. It is hard to find specific Bible examples for our daily journey. Here is what I have learned: I don't go too far wrong if I love others the way I wish I'd been loved.

We are not limited to how well our parents loved us. This is good news. At the end of the day, they are not our example of how to love. Jesus is. And his example is available for all to follow. Jesus loved people by speaking the truth, living the truth, setting captives free, and healing the sick, thus revealing the heart of the Father everywhere he went.

Love by Speaking the Truth

There are times when love means telling someone what they are missing. We all have gaps in our lives and blind spots we are unable to see. When we ask Jesus, he will tell us the truth about ourselves so that our hearts can be true.

When a rich and influential young man asked Jesus what he had to do to inherit eternal life, Jesus responded in love:

And Jesus, looking at him, loved him, and said to him, "You lack one thing: go, sell all that you have and give to the poor,

and you will have treasure in heaven; and come, follow me."
(Mark 10:21)

This man's "one thing" was everything. Jesus knew what
was needed to unlock this young man's imprisoned heart.
Your one thing might be forgiving someone or trusting that
God cares. Whatever it is, the Holy Spirit knows what is
needed to unlock your heart. Like many of us, this rich
young ruler was filled with potential, but he held his treasure
in the wrong place. His treasure needed to be transferred
to the very place his heart longed to be . . . eternity. Jesus
saw him, loved him, heard the cry of his
heart, and spoke the truth.

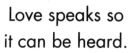

Love shows up in our words; it is evident in both what we say and what we
choose not to say. Love shows up in our

Love speaks so it can be heard.

tones. We've all said the right thing in the wrong spirit. I
have even managed to say the wrong thing with the right
spirit, which is still *no bueno*.

Love speaks so it can be heard.

At times love is a whisper, and other times love raises a
passionate shout. When we love . . . it will find its voice.

Love Lifts Others

Other times love means exposing how religion has twisted
the words and intention of the Father. Let's take a look at
Luke 13:

Now he was teaching in one of the synagogues on the
Sabbath. And behold, there was a woman who had had a

disabling spirit for eighteen years. She was bent over and could not fully straighten herself. (vv. 10–11)

For eighteen long, oppressive years, a disabling spirit had reduced the posture of this woman. This wasn't a blind spot; she knew she was bent. Maybe she had been told to try harder, to pray longer, to repent of sin. She felt the shame. She desperately wanted to be lifted but found no way to lift herself. She knew her presence made the synagogue leaders uncomfortable, but for eighteen years, she still came. She knew God was her only hope. Maybe you know just how she felt.

The young rabbi, Jesus, was teaching. She heard his words even though her stooped position limited her vantage. His words reached into her soul . . . tears moistened her downcast face. He paused. She did not know it yet, but Love had just noticed her. What was happening? Was he speaking to her? She strained her head sideways to see. His eyes were sounding the depth of her soul. The people around her parted as she shuffled forward amid the whispers.

When Jesus saw her, he called her over and said to her, "Woman, you are freed from your disability." And he laid his hands on her, and immediately she was made straight, and she glorified God. (vv. 12–13)

He didn't ask if she wanted freedom. He didn't ask the religious leaders for their permission. He touched her bent back. Her heart raced as strength came into her frame. Her chest opened up, her locked spine was pliable again, she rose to her full height and stretched her hands toward heaven. Unbidden cries of praise rose from her lips.

When Love saw her, he called her out, spoke freedom, release, and hope, and then touched her. Because we know that Jesus did only what he saw his Father do, this healing is a beautiful display of our Father's heart. Sadly, not everyone shared her joy.

> But the ruler of the synagogue, indignant because Jesus had healed on the Sabbath, said to the people, "There are six days in which work ought to be done. Come on those days and be healed, and not on the Sabbath day." (v. 14)

A woman was rejoicing and a leader was yelling. Work? When did healing become a work of men? It had always been the work of God! What better place for healing than the synagogue? Love had interrupted their religious pattern. Jesus fired back:

> You hypocrites! Does not each of you on the Sabbath untie his ox or his donkey from the manger and lead it away to water it? And ought not this woman, a daughter of Abraham whom Satan bound for eighteen years, be loosed from this bond on the Sabbath day? (vv. 15–16)

The release of this daughter stepped squarely on their religious toes. Do you think God ever intended oxen and donkeys to receive better treatment than his children? The Sabbath is for rest and restoration. Every form of oppression works against God's purpose for the Sabbath! This was a daughter of Abraham. The heart of God was moved to action because God is adamant about freeing his captive children.

> As he said these things, all his adversaries were put to shame, and all the people rejoiced at all the glorious things that were done by him. (v. 17)

Sadly, there are times when it is difficult to love religion and people at the same time. If you find yourself at this crossroads, choose to love people rather than the dogma of doctrine. Love has the ability to conquer lies and overcome deception, but hating and judging people will push them away. Faith works by love. There are times when love means telling the truth and other times when love means being the truth. In this passage, Jesus did both. By freeing this bound daughter, Jesus exemplified God's love for people over religious policy or practice.

> Just as faith without works is dead, works without love are meaningless.

Just as faith without works is dead, works without love are meaningless.

Action without Love

> If I speak in the tongues of men and of angels, but have not love, I am a noisy gong or a clanging cymbal. And if I have prophetic powers, and understand all mysteries and all knowledge, and if I have all faith, so as to remove mountains, but have not love, *I am nothing.* If I give away all I have, and if I deliver up my body to be burned, but have not love, *I gain nothing.* (1 Cor. 13:1–3)

There are a number of good things mentioned in the verses above that are incomplete without the factor of love. They include voice, knowledge, faith, and generosity. Any gift or talent we possess should point others to our generous Lord rather than draw them to ourselves. If you received the greatest gift you could imagine—a house, a car, or your college loan paid off in full—how would you feel and respond on the day the keys or the cash was placed in your hands? Wouldn't it only be natural for you to hug and thank the one who gave it to you? Is there any good thing we have that God has not given us? No, not a thing. Which is why our posture is gratitude, giving all that we have . . . even our very lives. But without love, our gifts add nothing.

Let's address these gifts Paul mentions, beginning with the power of voice.

Voice

We live in a day that is flooded with dynamic, persuasive, and winsome communicators. They come in every form and function; there are so many voices vying to be heard on so many fronts. It is hard to know what is behind all the speaking, typing, or broadcasting. Discernment begins with first tending the soil of our hearts. When we speak, we need to ask ourselves some hard questions.

"Am I speaking out of a place of love, or do I want to be seen and heard?" We all want to be heard. We all have the right to be heard. But when we speak out of hurt, pride, or the pursuit of popularity, being heard becomes its own reward.

Tending our hearts means the motive of love will not be lost in translation. Paul warns us that no matter how profound or divinely inspired our words might seem, without the factor of love, they will fall short like brash and irritating noises.

God alone knows the place from which we speak. In the same way that he sees beyond our appearance into our hearts, he hears more than our words . . . he hears the sound of their source. He hears the melodic or discordant tones in what we say. The simplest of sentences woven in love is a symphony. These three words . . . I am sorry . . . are incomparably lovely to him, while the most eloquent of speeches entwined with pride are like fingernails on a blackboard or the screech of banshees.

The following passage from Acts 12 is a case in point:

> On an appointed day Herod put on his royal robes, took his seat upon the throne, and delivered an oration to them. And the people were shouting, "*The voice of a god, and not of a man!*" Immediately an angel of the Lord struck him down, because he did not give God the glory, and he was eaten by worms and breathed his last. (vv. 21–23)

Yikes! Worship is reserved for God alone. When the royally robed Herod made the mistake of sharing God's glory, it was over. In a flash, he was struck down by an angel and consumed by worms. What an awful way to go! Many health professionals say that most of us have some presence of parasites . . . I know, sorry. If this is true, then what was unseen within him had its way with him. In light of this, it is no wonder that the apostles were so quick to tear their robes and reveal their humanity whenever they were mistaken for divinity. In Acts 14:14–15, we read:

> When the apostles understood what was happening, they were mortified and tore their clothes as a sign of dismay. They rushed into the crowd and shouted, "People, what are you doing? We're only weak human beings like everyone else. This is why we've come to tell you the good news, so that

you would turn away from these worthless myths and turn to the living God. He is the Creator of all things: the earth, the heavens, the sea, and everything they contain." (TPT)

It is interesting to note that when we back up a few verses in Acts 12 and look at the context of Herod's speech, we see that Herod not only gave a great speech but was also announcing an action of goodwill. Herod had been at odds with Tyre and Sidon, and as a result, he'd cut off their food supply. A delegation from Tyre and Sidon had come to negotiate peace and had found an ally in Blastus, Herod's personal assistant. The two cities were in desperate need of food. Herod's speech announced the reconciliation. The shift meant peace and a return to prosperity. Herod had been persuaded, but his motives were not pure.

Knowledge

The next gift mentioned in 1 Corinthians is the wondrous ability to predict the future, unravel life's secrets, and possess all knowledge. As wonderful as these are and as beneficial as they could be to the world at large, they add no value to the one who does not love. First Corinthians 8 describes the tension that can exist between love and knowledge:

This "knowledge" puffs up, but love builds up. If anyone imagines that he knows something, he does not yet know as he ought to know. But if anyone loves God, he is known by God. (vv. 1–3)

And to further highlight the relevance of this struggle, I've also pulled these verses from the TPT:

How easily we get puffed up over our opinions! But love builds up the structure of our new life. If anyone thinks of himself as a know-it-all, he still has a lot to learn. But if a person passionately loves God, he will possess the knowledge of God.

If the knowledge we possess isn't building up others, it's time to check our motives. Knowing more is an opportunity to love more. Knowing God well should always translate into loving others well.

Over the past few years, a number of spiritual daughters reached out to me. They didn't come to me for connections or speaking engagements. They invited me to speak into their lives on matters of love and life. There was no reason for them to make all the mistakes I already had. To that end, I used any understanding I'd gained to lift them higher. Love lifts the heart . . . without blowing up your head. Education and experience are not badges of merit that give us permission to make others feel like they are less than us. That is how the teachers of the law and the Pharisees wore knowledge. Knowledge without love has little merit.

> Knowing God well should always translate into loving others well.

A greater knowledge of who we are in Christ works its way out in us as we lift others. The dynamic "to know as we ought to know" means loving others in the manner that Christ loves them.

Love never demeans.

Love never shows off.

Love attacks the stronghold that holds the captive.

Love does not attack the captive; love sets the captive free.

We can know about love without being loving, just as we can embrace the concept of love without embracing people. We are called to love *everyone*. We cannot choose to love just those who look and act like us. We must love those who disagree with us. This does not mean we compromise our beliefs or confuse others with our actions. Somehow our culture has equated loving with approving. There are times that the most loving thing we can do is lovingly disagree. This is the tightrope of our day. We must daily choose to live with a sensitive awareness of other people.

Rather than being defined, love should be demonstrated. It is not hard to recognize love when we see it. Love is not a feeling; it is a way of life. In many ways, love is the greatest habit that any of us could develop.

And one of the scribes came up and heard them disputing with one another, and seeing that he answered them well, asked him, "Which commandment is the most important of all?" Jesus answered, "The most important is, 'Hear, O Israel: The Lord our God, the Lord is one. And you shall love the Lord your God with all your heart and with all your soul and with all your mind and with all your strength.' The second is this: 'You shall love your neighbor as yourself.' There is no other commandment greater than these." And the scribe said to him, "You are right, Teacher. You have truly said that he is one, and there is no other besides him. And to love him with all the heart and with all the understanding and with all the strength, and to love one's neighbor as oneself, is much more than all whole burnt offerings and sacrifices." And when Jesus saw that he answered wisely, he said to him, "You are not far from the kingdom of God." And after that no one dared to ask him any more questions. (Mark 12:28–34)

Even today, in many ways, we are not far from the kingdom of God. We see it in the distance, and yet there is a gaping chasm between what we believe and how the church behaves. Love is the answer that puts an end to all questions. It is the solution to all problems.

Owe no one anything, except to love each other, for the one who loves another has fulfilled the law. (Rom. 13:8)

Love fulfills the law. Love frees us of all emotional, physical, and social debts. We owe only what we have been so freely given . . . love.

Be watchful, stand firm in the faith, act like men [and women], be strong. Let all that you do be done in love. (1 Cor. 16:13–14)

The ideas in these two verses in 1 Corinthians are related. It takes maturity, faith, consistency, vigilance, and strength to assure that what we do is done in love.

Love moves us to action. Recently, I was at a concert where there was an opportunity to sponsor a child through Compassion. As an organization, we partner with orphans on a regular basis. This time I felt the need to personally respond. I threw up my hand and received a packet. I looked down and realized I held in my hand the photo of a little girl who shares the same birthday as me. What were the chances? Her photo is now perched on my shelf over my laptop. That act of love has been like a kiss on the cheek from my Father.

Each day is another chance to love.

Each day is another chance to love.

And because God loves people, he never wants our freedom to hinder his love from reaching them. Love is mindful of how our choices affect others. In 1 Corinthians 8, Paul gives a lengthy explanation of the revelation that even though idols are nothing, eating food sacrificed to idols can potentially offend new believers who do not yet have this revelation. In verses 11 and 12, he explains the fruit of revelation without love:

> So in effect, by exercising your understanding of freedom, you have ruined this weak believer, a brother for whom Christ has died. And when you offend weaker believers by wounding their consciences in this way, you also offend the Anointed One! (TPT)

And what was love's response to all of this?

> So I conclude that if my eating certain food deeply offends my brother and hinders his advance in Christ, I will never eat it again. I don't want to be guilty of causing my brother or sister to be wounded and defeated. (1 Cor. 8:13 TPT)

This verse personifies how love chooses to live *on behalf* of others. Knowledge on its own would say, "Because the idol is nothing, I am free to eat as I please. I'm not responsible for my brother's reaction." When knowledge is coupled with love, it will look for ways to advance the lives of others. This pairing says, "I know the idol is nothing, but to my brother and sister, it is something. I care more about them than my right to exercise freedom. I would never want my actions of freedom to put them at risk." Love restrains itself to build up others.

Having said this, love doesn't mean we live *controlled by* the fears and opinions of others. Rather, love lives aware.

————◇————

Love never wields its freedom to wound the weak.

The topic of eating meat sacrificed to idols is all but unknown to us in our culture, but in the early church it was a very real and sensitive matter. New converts in Greece found it difficult to reconcile their former rituals with their new lives. Those with a revelation of the one true God realized that love meant honoring the sensitivity of others. Love never wields its freedom to wound the weak.

Faith

C. S. Lewis says, "Do not waste time bothering whether you 'love' your neighbor; act as if you did. As soon as we do this we find one of the great secrets. When you are behaving as if you loved someone you will presently come to love him."[1]

When we love by faith, and we love in faith, the hurting world sees the Father's heart. It is more important to love than to be loved. The truest measure of our faith is not found in how well loved we are but in how well we love. Yes, we all want to be loved. When we receive the Father's adamant love for us, then we are well positioned in him to love others. Loving like this takes faith. We know that faith is the substance of things hoped for. We all hope to love and be loved, but none of us can truly love without faith. Galatians 5:6 tells us, "For in Christ Jesus neither circumcision [law] nor uncircumcision counts for anything, but *only faith working through love.*"

There is no use trying to separate faith and love . . . they are forever intimately intertwined. God knew it would be impossible to follow Christ and love the way he loves in our own strength or ability, so he gave each of us a measure of faith. Love is not for the faint of heart. Faith means we can love even when we don't feel love.

> You have heard that it was said, "You must love your neighbor" and hate your enemy. But I say to you, love your enemies and pray for those who persecute you. (Matt. 5:43–44 ISV)

At first glance, the Old Testament approach makes complete sense: hate your enemy and love your neighbor . . . check. But let's probe a bit deeper. If you have been married more than a year, you probably know there are times when it takes faith to love your spouse. When John and I were first married, we would have ridiculous arguments late at night. Exhausted, we would go to bed lying as far away from each other as possible, and we would close our night with, "I forgive you by faith!"

At the time, it was our way of saying, "I know I should forgive you, but I'm not ready to let it go, so I'm doing it by faith." I wasn't drawing on faith; it was nothing more than a religious jab at my husband. My heart was in the wrong place, but it is possible that the principle was correct.

Forgiving someone by faith is a vote of confidence that better days are ahead. It is also an act of surrender. We received forgiveness by faith, therefore we can give forgiveness by faith.

If you are part of a family, there will be moments when you will have to love your siblings by faith. If you go to church, any church, anywhere, there will be people in the congregation you will have to love by faith. I have friends I love by faith! (And thankfully, they do the same for me.) But the love of Jesus didn't stop with our neighbors.

Jesus moved beyond the realm of the difficult and threw wide the door to the impossible. He told us to love our enemies. We all have enemies. I wish it weren't so, but enemies are a fact of life. Knowing this doesn't make it any easier to love them. Loving an enemy definitely requires faith. It is not easy to turn the other cheek when an enemy's hand is poised to strike you again. The first slap may have been unexpected, but when you know what's coming, it takes faith not to block the next strike or slap back—especially if you are half Sicilian.

It takes faith to speak a blessing to those who out of jealousy or spite choose to curse, malign, and criticize you. (These principles apply to real life and to social media!) It takes faith to do good to people who hate you. And it takes faith to pray with any form of sincerity for those who misuse and persecute you. I am not encouraging you to allow abusers access—don't do it! I am telling you to love them from a safe distance by faith through prayer. Jesus loved all, but don't confuse loving well with trusting all.

> Our love opens their hearts to God's love.

It helps to have an awareness that we are not actually wrestling with what we see but with dark, unseen forces. And it also helps to know we don't wrestle alone.

Relying on the deep wisdom of my Logos software, I was able to compile a good working definition of love found in the Greek word *agape*: it is choosing actions of love even when they are undeserved and coupled with rejection and disappointment. Love functions independently of our preferences or inclinations. This definition is the fundamentals of love.

People sense when we love them, and our love opens their hearts to God's love. They know when they are noticed by love or if we simply want to change them. Having received such an adamant love from our Father, we are to love as we have been loved.

Fearlessly: because there is no fear in love.

Selflessly: because love is not selfish.

Free of offense: because love is not easily offended.

Triumphantly: because love never fails.

Endlessly: because love is eternal.

If nations loved their neighbors as themselves, then nation would not rise up against nation. There would be no wars or even rumors of wars. Most of our challenges arise when we try to establish peace outside the realm of the Prince of Peace.

For far too long, our nation has been torn by a spirit of racism. All prejudice thrives on anger and ignorance, but don't imagine that the spirit behind it is stupid. It has a strategic purpose and an origin as ancient as the Garden of Eden. When Adam and Eve fell, their actions set into motion a series of divisions. One of these plays out as brother against brother. Racism is a ploy of the serpent. It must be given no place and no tolerance. Every Christian everywhere must denounce every form of racism and do whatever they can to end it.

Generosity

Finally, in 1 Corinthians 13:3, Paul lists acts of unmitigated generosity, such as giving away *all* our possessions to the poor and the unthinkable act of submitting our bodies to the flames of agonizing martyrdom, and tells the church that if such acts are not motivated by love, they will add nothing to the giver.

He is driving his point home:

Everything – Love = Nothing

Without love, we are nothing.

Without love, we add nothing.

God is adamant that love be the reason behind all we do.

This is a sobering picture. In all honesty, only eternity will accurately weigh our motives in this matter. I readily admit that my own life may have an alarming heap of words and deeds void of eternal value. There is no reason you should not learn from my mistakes. Like the diamond that evaporated under the intense magnification of heat and oxygen, our works will one day be refined by the intense light of God's presence as our motives are revealed.

> God is adamant that love be the reason behind all we do.

Diamonds Aren't Forever

Even as my hands hover over the keys, there is a different diamond ring on my left hand. Somehow in the course of my crazy life, I managed to break my first one. So in Sicily on my forty-eighth birthday, John surprised me again, this time with an oval-shaped diamond.

A flaw ultimately fractured my tear-shaped stone. It was poised to tumble from its setting when I turned it over to the insurance company. But I felt so sentimental about the diamond that I bought the splintered stone back. I hope to one day have the fractured diamond cut and reset for one of my granddaughters so it might begin a new story.

Thirty-five years is a long time to be married.

I won't pretend to have loved my husband perfectly . . . I haven't.

There were difficult seasons when we both felt hopeless. There were harsh words and stretches of time when our love felt like a broken diamond. Times when I looked at our love and didn't see radiance or promises but only sharp edges. But we didn't stay in our despair. We grew.

We are still not perfect, but we are strong and healthy. We are adamantly committed to loving each other well. We ask for help and go to counseling to gain tools and insight. This concept of well means that when we make mistakes, we move forward by choosing to learn from them. As we have matured, we have made sure our commitment to love rather than conflict defines our relationship. No one gains when we hold debts and demand payment from each other.

Over the course of the years, we have chosen to extract the lessons love would teach us from our infractions. Just as in any relationship, there were times when John was more to blame and other times when I was. Relationships should never be about tipping the scales in one direction or the other to measure fault. There is rarely a time or a relationship in which I could be blamed for being too loving. We always have room to grow when it comes to love.

I want to love my husband more rather than be more in love with him. (Okay, that would be nice too.) I've learned it is dangerous to allow my feelings to direct my actions. Like a dog on a leash, our feelings must be trained to follow our actions. Which ultimately means love is a choice.

John wants to love me well. We want to show our love for God by loving each other well. Even though we both share this desire, it doesn't come to fruition by putting more demands on each other. I learned this lesson early in life.

My parents had a very difficult marriage. I remember coming home from school and there on the refrigerator in the midst of coupons, school schedules, and our list of chores was a contract. It was an itemized list of all the changes my mother expected from my father. Drawing on her skills as a real estate agent, she had created what appeared to be a legally binding document. There was even a closing date by which time his behavior needed to be amended. Both of my parents had signed the document. My mother had reached a critical point, and her stipulations would be considered reasonable in a healthy marriage. But my parents' marriage was desperately wounded. Did I mention my father was an alcoholic and 100 percent Sicilian? The document remained on display even when friends or family visited.

I didn't have to wait for the appointed time. Even at twelve, I knew my father would fail on purpose and my mother would hold him accountable so that they both could escape a loveless marriage. The countdown had begun, and in a matter of months, my parents were divorced.

Without love, even clearly communicated expectations are impossible to meet. Whether it is in a friendship, a family relationship, or a marriage, love factors in mercy and grace. The law could not have been clearer when it came to both God's expectations and his hope for us, and yet we failed. Even so, there were always those who pressed in beyond the letter of the law and experienced God's goodness. Women such as Rahab and Ruth and men such as David and Abraham were able to keep God's law with their hearts even as their lives fell short. It is no accident that these are some of the giants in the faith, because faith works by love.

And hope does not put us to shame, because God's love has been poured into our hearts through the Holy Spirit who has been given to us. (Rom. 5:5)

When we love, it is not merely heard; it is seen.

Love Reaches Out

Do you miss phone calls? I do. I miss the sound of people's voices, their tones and inflections. Recently, I felt impressed to call someone. It was a beautiful young woman I was getting ready to do a conference with. The moment she answered the phone I knew she was crying. We talked. We prayed. In that moment, she needed a living, breathing person. If I had only looked at her social media, I never would have guessed her pain. You can't hear someone cry in a photo.

Social media is a network. It was never meant to replace human touch or conversation. Use it to foster your relationships rather than replace them.

Speaking to an audience through social networks doesn't mean we can neglect our face-to-face conversations. Doing both well is hard. If you have to choose between the two, speak to the people you can see. I'm truly concerned we're creating a voyeuristic celebrity culture that builds virtual walls that leave many people feeling left out.

Let's build fences rather than walls. This means constructing boundaries rather than barriers. The phrase "good fences make good neighbors" was about respecting one another's land, livestock, and property lines. Fences were built to keep livestock in rather than people out. Split rail fences divide fields while maintaining an open line of sight. When it comes to

◇

Love requires closeness.

social media, we need to put some split rail fences in place. These are the type of boundaries we can climb through, over, and even under, while at the same time they keep us safe from raging bulls.

Let's not spend so much time talking to the masses that we lose the art of speaking to one another. Call someone. Knock on a door. Hug someone.

Talk to strangers . . . you're already doing it on social media. Talk to real, live people in the grocery store. Touch their arm. Lean over and kiss your husband, your child, your grandchild. Tickle them and make them put down their iPad or cell phone. When they ask to watch a show, take them for a walk instead. Look people in the eyes and see them. It is easy to hate from afar, but love requires closeness. Jesus is our pattern, and he was never afraid to draw nearer.

Becoming Adamant in Love

I know it's a lot of verses, but the following passage from Romans is a brilliant outline of how to love others. Be affectionate, honoring, fervent, hopeful, patient, constant, generous, hospitable, never vengeful, empathetic, humble, peaceable, and aware of the needs of your enemies. Let's love, with God's help, as we have been loved.

Let's turn Romans 12 into our prayer by asking the Holy Spirit to show us the places where our hearts need to be unlocked.

Dear heavenly Father,
I want to love how you love. I choose to . . .

Love one another with brotherly affection. Outdo one another in showing honor. Do not be slothful in zeal, be fervent in spirit, serve the Lord. Rejoice in hope, be patient in tribulation, be constant in prayer. Contribute to the needs of the saints and seek to show hospitality. Bless those who persecute you; bless and do not curse them. Rejoice with those who rejoice, weep with those who weep. Live in harmony with one another. Do not be haughty, but associate with the lowly. Never be wise in your own sight. Repay no one evil for evil, but give thought to do what is honorable in the sight of all. If possible, so far as it depends on you, live peaceably with all. Beloved, never avenge yourselves, but leave it to the wrath of God, for it is written, "Vengeance is mine, I will repay, says the Lord." To the contrary, "if your enemy is hungry, feed him; if he is thirsty, give him something to drink; for by so doing you will heap burning coals on his head." Do not be overcome by evil, but overcome evil with good. (Rom. 12:10–21)

6

ADAMANT IN HATE

We cannot love God without hating that which
he hates.

Charles Spurgeon

I know. This is a tough one. It totally caught me off guard
as well, but it is just not possible to love God unless we
hate what he hates. Let me share how the tension between these two became a reality for me. I had just finished
writing the previous chapters on love when I heard the Holy
Spirit whisper, "Lisa, I am also adamant in hate."

My heart skipped a beat.

How could our God who is love . . . hate?

As though in answer, a phrase from Proverbs came to mind:
"There are six things that the LORD hates . . ." Well, there it
was. It wasn't a passage I referenced often, so I opened up
my Bible software and copied and pasted four verses from
Proverbs 6 into a new document and called it a day.

We were vacationing in Florida with eleven people crammed into one house, so I was writing in a friend's carriage house and had left my cell phone behind. When I got back to the house, I had a number of text messages.

One of them was from my friend Rabbi Brian. He said that the Holy Spirit had shown him I was writing, and he encouraged me to pursue the fresh line of thought that had come to me that day. Without knowing what it was, he assured me "it was the antidote to counteract the poison that has inoculated the church with secular deception instead of the sacred wisdom of the Scriptures." He went on to say, "We have no time in this crucial and critical hour to be seduced by the selfish and insecure need for acceptance among the world and to fit into society's dysfunctional definition of what a believer is bound to be like instead of letting the *image* of God determine whom we resemble and the *likeness* of God to define how we function and operate in the earth." Well, then, there you go.

God hates all that unmakes love.

The next morning before I sat down to type or even search the Scriptures, I prayed, "Heavenly Father, I need you to speak to me. My first reaction is that hate is irreconcilable with a God who is love, yet I see clearly from Proverbs that there are in fact things you hate. Teach me. In Jesus's name, amen."

No sooner had amen passed my lips than the Holy Spirit began to speak. I scribbled down what I heard as quickly as it came. Here are the highlights of what I hope to explore in this chapter:

God hates all that unmakes love.

God hates what unmakes and breaks those he loves.

God hates what undermines his image and distorts our identity.

In short, our Father hates all that perverts and corrupts love. God loves people. God loves the broken. God loves the bound. God loves the sinner. God is love, and love never hates people, because people are who God loves.

God loves every *one* . . . but God does not love every *thing*.

In the genesis of creation, God made all things good and for our good. Sadly, I don't need to tell you that we no longer walk the uncorrupted soil of Eden. The very earth below our feet groans, aching for its restoration. In the same way, every human heart is filled with a desperate longing for the revelation and the realization of all that is true, just, and beautiful. We want to see love gain its full expression in every area of life. Is it possible that we have idolized love and in the process called things love that are not? Have we believed our actions were loving when in actuality they were not? God is love, but love is not God. We worship God, not love. Nothing can separate us from the love of God in Christ Jesus (Rom. 8:39). But danger arises when we separate love from the parameters of our God.

God is love (1 John 4:8). God is a consuming fire (Heb. 12:29). In him we live (Acts 17:28). When we pull these truths together, it is not a stretch to say, "We live in the consuming fire of God's love."

Why Hate?

Hatred is an emotionally charged negative word. There is absolutely nothing neutral about hate. I immediately think of the word association: hate crimes. To explore this path with me, I need you to step away from your personal experiences with hate and disassociate the word from all people. For the duration of these pages and for the purpose of navigating truth, push aside the images and the hateful actions. Do you agree that the definition of love has been distorted by both our culture and human experiences? Do you agree that the term *love* has been misused? Far too often people say they love without the corresponding actions or the commitment of love. When a word is overused, its meaning can be cheapened or even lost. To truly love as God loves, we cannot love what he hates.

Just as love cannot be defined outside our Creator's eternal perspective, so too we must look to the Scriptures for a definition of hate. For the moment, let's push aside our human *experiences* with hate and deal with its *meaning*.

As a noun, it encompasses such hostile words as animosity, abhorrence, revulsion, and disgust. When hate adopts the form of a verb, it means to loathe, detest, be repulsed by, and despise.

At first glance, it is easy to assume that none of these attributes are in step with a God who not only loves but also is love. Yet as I searched the Scriptures, I discovered the following. Our Father hates:

everything that undermines justice and truth
when widows, orphans, and aliens are oppressed
the abuse of the elderly and the neglect of family
what perverts his goodness and taints his gifts
when love twists into selfishness and friends become
    enemies
what changes his image and distorts ours

when evil is called good and the innocent are killed

when arrogance and pride degrade us

These points are a general overview, not an exhaustive list. The best frame of reference is that God hates all that undermines love, for everything that debases love debases us.

As I searched the Scriptures to gain an understanding of what God hates, I was shocked to discover more than three thousand words that give context to things that degrade what love seeks to build.

When love is debased, our understanding of God, who is love, is tragically undermined. When God's image is distorted, children who seek a Father are confused. Ultimately, everything God hates is about protecting what he loves. Why was I surprised? Every loving parent hates every form of vice that would seek to destroy their children. The Old Testament is not the words of an angry God; rather, it is the admonition of a loving Father who wanted his children to live life at their best. Jesus didn't change God's mind in the New Testament. Jesus came to reveal the Father's heart.

> **God hates all that undermines love, for everything that debases love debases us.**

No parent wants hardship for their children. Yet struggles and challenges are not our ultimate enemy. Earthly trials can serve as crucibles that drive God's children to a place of humility and prayer. Challenges give us fresh eyes that translate into new perspectives as we read the Word of God. Our true enemies are of a more subtle nature. They are vices such as greed, pride, compromise, immorality, idolatry, and depravity. These distortions of life lie to the children of God by implying that we can serve two masters: God and this world's system.

Let's be honest, a generation has arrived hungry in the wilderness. They wander the ancient paths again, disappointed with what they have seen in marriage, in our government, and even in their houses of worship. In this season of hunger, the enemy has seized them and taken them to lofty peaks and promised the world to them if they would simply bow and worship at his altar of self. Our culture echoes his resound as it encourages us to make peace where there can be no peace and call holy things that are not. Our culture appeals to our intellect and invites us to deny the limits of the antiquated text and the ancient words of what is perceived to be a now-silent God.

> A generation has arrived hungry in the wilderness.

Hating the Light

To truly love light, we must be willing to risk being hated by darkness. To be loved by the world, we must love what it loves. But the acceptance doesn't stop there. We must likewise hate what the world hates. If we do not do both, then we will be hated. We must endorse what the world system endorses or there will be a cry of foul.

> The Light of God has now come into the world, but the hearts of people love their darkness more than the Light, because they want the darkness to conceal their evil. So the wicked hate the Light and try to hide from it, for their lives

are fully exposed in the Light. But those who love the truth will come out into the Light and welcome its exposure, for the Light will reveal that their fruitful works were produced by God. (John 3:19–21 TPT)

When we are afraid of exposure, it is easier to choose to love our darkness and blame the light for its exposing tendencies. Some choose to call the darkness light. I get it. It's not fun to be called out, but at times it is healthy. Eventually, *everything* hidden within the folds of darkness will be brought into the light. Better to allow the Holy Spirit to address every shadowed place now. Don't be afraid. We have the assurance that even the darkness is light to him.

If I say, "Surely the darkness shall cover me,
  and the light about me be night,"
even the darkness is not dark to you;
  the night is bright as the day,
  for darkness is as light with you. (Ps. 139:11–12)

The Holy Spirit can light our way and counsel us along our paths. The only way to tackle our fear is to invite the light into every area of our lives. When we decide to hate everything that shadows the soul by embracing the light, we will turn from what it reveals. Love flourishes in an undivided heart; therefore, God hates what divides our affections. The early church understood this. Read the impassioned plea of the apostle James, the brother of Jesus:

You have become spiritual adulterers who are having an affair, an unholy relationship with the world. Don't you know that flirting with the world's values places you at odds with God? Whoever chooses to be the world's friend makes himself God's enemy! Does the Scripture mean nothing to you that says, "The Spirit that God breathed into our hearts is a jealous Lover who desires to have us fully"? (James 4:4–5 TPT)

There are those who would argue that these verses are not for us today. They reason that we have evolved to a higher place. And yet when I look around, I can't remember a time when I have seen humanity sunk so low. Heaven has a very different value system than this earth's. Therefore, we are warned against even flirting with the world's values.

Heaven has a very different value system than this earth's.

When I began to research what our God of love hates, the search began with Proverbs 6, so let's examine it together:

> There are six things that the LORD hates,
>   seven that are an abomination to him:
> haughty eyes, a lying tongue,
>   and hands that shed innocent blood,
> a heart that devises wicked plans,
>   feet that make haste to run to evil,
> a false witness who breathes out lies,
>   and one who sows discord among brothers. (vv. 16–19)

And here is a closer look at the seven.

Pride

God hates pride because it sets us in opposition to the transformative power of love. The book of James tells us that God actually resists and opposes the proud while gracing the humble and the teachable (James 4:6).

In *Mere Christianity*, C. S. Lewis wrote, "For pride is spiritual cancer: it eats up the very possibility of love, or contentment, or even common sense."[1] Of course our Father couldn't help but hate such a singularly undermining enemy of our transformation.

To paint a visual of pride, Proverbs 6:17 uses the words "haughty eyes." These look down on others in a manner of contempt. The Passion Translation spells it out a bit further: "putting others down while considering yourself superior." And yet isn't that the very look that is modeled for us in almost every form of advertisement or fashion magazine?

Here are a few more passages that elaborate on the destructive outworkings of pride:

> The fear of the LORD is hatred of evil.
> Pride and arrogance and the way of evil
>   and perverted speech I hate. (Prov. 8:13)

Pride will eventually pervert our speech and take us down the path of evil.

> Haughty eyes and a proud heart,
>   the lamp of the wicked, are sin. (Prov. 21:4)

This verse tells us sin is behind the enlightenment of pride that darkens the understanding of the wicked.

> If you try to correct an arrogant cynic, expect an angry insult in return. And if you try to confront an evil man, don't be surprised if all you get is a slap in the face! So don't even bother to correct a mocker, for he'll only hate you for it. But

go ahead and correct the wise; they'll love you even more. (Prov. 9:7–8 TPT)

Pride makes us defensive, aggressive, and blind to our true condition. Cynicism and arrogance are bedfellows of pride. Pride considers any instruction to be an affront. Correction is never fun, but we can learn to love the fruit of correction: wisdom.

To love what our Father loves, we must first close the door to pride because it acts as a gateway to destruction.

Lying

A lying tongue includes both the act of lying and the spreading of rumors. My friend, in our day and age, we cannot be too careful about what we choose to say, repeat, and post. Trolls are no longer make-believe; they are very real. They no longer hide under bridges—they travel the information highway and rob people of their good names even as they sow strife and dissension.

A good rule of thumb is this: if you don't know, let it go. God hates the act of intentionally slandering and lying. Proverbs 12:22 tells us, "Lying lips are an abomination to the LORD, but those who act faithfully are his delight." This makes the point that lying is often a cover for unfaithfulness. God is the author and originator of truth. When we lie, we behave like our former overseer, Satan, who is the father of lies, for truth does not live in him. Lies curse love. Lying is not loving. And here is the most frightening thing about lying: when we lie long enough, we lose touch with the truth and actually deceive ourselves.

> ◇
> **Lying is not loving.**

Innocent Bloodshed

The phrase "hands that shed innocent blood" describes the premeditated or perverse desire to kill the innocent. In the time period when the book of Proverbs was authored, this referred to the widespread practice of child sacrifice by the worshipers of Baal-Molech and Ashtoreth that had also infected the Israelites (1 Kings 14). This worship included sexual orgies. The infants conceived through this practice were sacrificed to the flames of Molech, their piercing screams muffled by the sound of the pagan priests beating drums. It seems unthinkable that a mother could throw her living infant into the flames, yet the prophet Isaiah speaks of this practice:

> You satisfy your lust any place you find some shade and fornicate at whim. You kill your children at any convenient spot—any cave or crevasse will do. . . . You've climbed a high mountain to practice your foul sex-and-death religion. Behind closed doors you assemble your precious gods and goddesses. Deserting me, you've gone all out, stripped down and made your bed your place of worship. (57:5, 7–8 Message)

Have we made our beds of promiscuity our place of worship only to have innocent children pay the price?

Today there are no drums and caves. We are more civilized than that. Innocent blood is shed in the silence of the mother's womb. The mother has the choice of being asleep or awake during her "procedure." Killing the baby in utero means neither the mother nor the father need hear or see the death of the child. For nearly fifty years, our nation has sanctioned the widespread practice of abortion. Proponents of abortion have been known to call it a woman's "sacred ritual" and "sacrament."[2] It has even been argued as a "religious freedom." God help us. We choose to hate the act, not the people involved. Love supports the brave young women who choose to give life, as well as works to redeem the ones who shed innocent blood.

Hearts That Devise Wicked Plans

A heart that devises wicked plans refers to the willful, premeditated plotting of evil to harm another. God has a plan for our lives. It is a plan for good and not for harm. It is the very reason we are told to bless rather than curse those who abuse and mistreat us. When we plan evil for others, we are in opposition to the will of God for their lives and ours.

Feet That Run to What Is Evil

The Bible is very clear that evil is something to turn and run from rather than move toward. Instead of running, the Passion Translation of Proverbs 6:18 describes this in terms we can more readily understand: those who are "gloating over doing what is plainly wrong." Some people are proud of what they get away with. They imagine themselves crafty if they aren't caught. What they fail to recognize is that even if every earthly eye is blinded, there is One who yet sees.

> Even if every earthly eye is blinded, there is One who yet sees.

False Witnesses

I was surprised that Proverbs 6 lists both a lying tongue and a false witness among the things God hates. Aren't they almost the same thing? When I researched the difference, I learned that a false witness is one who lies under oath. They are not merely lying to men; they are lying to God and in the process perverting the course of justice. Our just God hates injustice. It is the very reason we take this oath in American courtrooms: "I swear that the evidence I give shall be the truth, the whole truth, and nothing but the truth, so help me God." God is the ultimate Judge. Therefore, when we pervert justice with false testimony, we undermine the foundation of God's plan for justice for all (see also Exod. 18:21; Prov. 17:15).

Sowing Discord among Brothers

God also hates sowing discord among brothers. I'm pretty sure that even though Proverbs 6 says "brothers," sisters could be factored into this one as well. The opposite of discord is accord, which means agreement, harmony, and unity. King David offers the antidote for falling under the corrupting spell of those who sow discord:

> I do not sit with men of falsehood,
>   nor do I consort with hypocrites.
> I hate the assembly of evildoers,
>   and I will not sit with the wicked.
> I wash my hands in innocence
>   and go around your altar, O LORD,
> proclaiming thanksgiving aloud,
>   and telling all your wondrous deeds.
> O LORD, I love the habitation of your house
>   and the place where your glory dwells.
>   (Ps. 26:4–8)

We avoid the association of liars, hypocrites, and evildoers by loving God and loving the house of God. As we gather, an attitude of gratefulness is heightened and God's faithfulness and wonder are proclaimed. Talking about God can clear some rooms as quickly as it fills others.

That completes the list from Proverbs 6—but there are more things God hates.

Sexual Immorality, Impurity, and Idolatry

For you may be sure of this, that everyone who is sexually immoral or impure, or who is covetous (that is, an idolater), has no inheritance in the kingdom of Christ and God. Let no one deceive you with empty words, for because of these things the wrath of God comes upon the sons of disobedience. (Eph. 5:5–6)

God can't help but hate the things that undermine our intimacy or deceive, debase, defile, and destroy us. These three—sexual immorality (all sexual activity contrary to biblical principles), impurity (filthy, coarse, lewd language and practices), and idolatry (greed and covetousness)—are almost inseparable. We see them merged seamlessly in the majority of what our culture calls entertainment.

I was once trapped next to a man who watched *Game of Thrones* for fourteen hours from LA to Sydney. (It was one of those times I was thankful I had vision in only one eye.) I felt defiled by what I just happened to see when I turned my head or climbed over him to go to the bathroom. He was utterly oblivious. When these three are packaged well and paraded in front of us often enough, they are normalized. Sadly, we will begin to emulate what entertains us.

Greed

Scripture refers to the vice of greed as covetousness and idolatry. I have heard it said that an unhealthy relationship with money (covetousness) is very dangerous because money has the ability to make us feel like gods. We imagine ourselves powerful and that anything we want is within our grasp. Why trust God when we have buying power? Greed and covetousness are often cloaked as subtle vices and therefore they are much more socially acceptable. Don't be fooled. Greed is a cruel captor that tricks people into imagining themselves free (Rev. 3:7–18). Captives of greed will value their relationships with possessions and position above their relationships with people. Generosity and humility are the antidotes to covetousness and idolatry.

Jesus warned his disciples, "No servant can serve two masters, for either he will hate the one and love the other, or he will be devoted to the one and despise the other. You cannot serve God and money" (Luke 16:13).

Money is a tool to be used . . . not loved. People are to be loved . . . not used—which brings us to the next point.

Divorce

"For I hate divorce!" says the LORD, the God of Israel. "To divorce your wife is to overwhelm her with cruelty," says the Lord of Heaven's Armies. "So guard your heart; do not be unfaithful to your wife." (Mal. 2:16 NLT)

The pain of divorce is bitter and intimate. This is the reason God hates it. He doesn't hate those who have divorced . . . he hates the rending of divorce. In the days of Malachi, women did not have the right to divorce their husbands. Imagine the angst of our heavenly Father as he saw his beloved covenant daughters rejected and abandoned by the very sons he hoped would love them. This displacement often happened in favor of foreign wives. God hated the violence and shame this practice inflicted on his daughters. The New International Version says that a man who divorces his wife "does violence to the one he should protect" (Mal. 2:16).

We live in a time when women can likewise divorce their husbands. Sometimes due to the betrayal of unfaithfulness and the pain of abuse, a spouse (male or female) will feel that divorce is the healthiest choice for their life and the safety of their children. In these cases, divorce is a provision for preventing something else God hates . . . a woman who is married and unloved (Prov. 30:23). When we dig deeper, we find that God's hatred of divorce is attached to our hardhearted mistreatment of one another.

In marriage, God weaves us together by his Spirit to make us one:

> Didn't the Lord make you one with your wife? In body and spirit you are his. And what does he want? Godly children from your union. So guard your heart; remain loyal to the wife of your youth. (Mal. 2:15 NLT)

The union of marriage foreshadows the union of Christ and his bride. Divorces initiated out of selfishness, unfaithfulness, and rejection distort the idea of God as a husband who will never leave or neglect us.

God does not want there to be any confusion about his adamant love for us. He has no intention of failing to protect the covenant he has made with us. He will never put us away or overwhelm us with cruelty. No matter how many times we may disappoint him, he can never disappoint us.

Though provision was made for divorce under the law, our God is a faithful husband to his bride. Divorce undermines the imagery of Christ and his church, of our Bridegroom who is always faithful even when we are faithless.

God knows—and we know—that divorce has a history of rending families and hearts. God makes provision because he hates the cruel abuse of unfaithfulness and abandonment, but divorce was never his original hope for the covenant of marriage.

Double Standards and Hypocrisy

To set high standards for someone else, and then not live up to them yourself, is something that God truly hates. But it pleases him when we apply the right standards of measurement. (Prov. 11:1 TPT)

The Lord hates double standards. That's hypocrisy at its worst! (Prov. 20:23 TPT)

Jesus constantly confronted the hypocrisy of the Pharisees. He was busy about his Father's business, building the kingdom of heaven, while they were busy enacting the laws of the kingdom of men. They held everyone to high standards they did not live up to themselves. Their duplicity muddied waters that were meant to be clear. As we learned earlier, they believed it was an affront to heal on the Sabbath. One was a sign of the covenant, and the other spoke of its wonder. Jesus warned his followers in Matthew 23:2–4:

The scribes and the Pharisees sit on Moses' seat, so do and observe whatever they tell you, but not the works they do. *For they preach, but do not practice.* They tie up heavy burdens, hard to bear, and lay them on people's shoulders, but they themselves are not willing to move them with their finger.

We will be forever doomed to preach without the ability to practice if our motive is to be *seen* by others rather than to *lift* others. Religions that are infiltrated by pride and hypocrisy oppress their adherents. Hypocritical leaders believe that pushing others lower will raise them higher. This is the antithesis of how God's kingdom operates. We bend before him that he might lift us. Once lifted, we bend again to raise others. In all honesty, more people have had the benefit of learning from my failures than from any of my so-called successes.

Before we get all excited about hating the hypocrisy of others, let's ask the Holy Spirit to reveal any traces of its taint in ourselves. Hypocrisy can slip in on all of us with great stealth. I have found that the only thing that uproots it is God's Word. The light of its truth rightly divides our motives and exposes any darkness that may have slipped in when we were unaware. Be vigilant against this enemy. It is insidious. Hypocrisy hates honesty, so intentionally surround yourself with truth tellers. Be vulnerable with the right people and ask them for honest input. (Sorry, but this is not going to happen on Facebook.)

> **We bend before him that he might lift us.**

The Rejection of Wisdom

Wisdom: you either love it or hate it. The way to learn to love wisdom begins by choosing to love what we naturally hate: discipline. Listen to the words of wisdom:

> How long, O simple ones, will you love being simple? How long will scoffers delight in their scoffing and fools hate knowledge? If you turn at my reproof, behold, I will pour out my spirit to you; I will make my words known to you. (Prov. 1:22–23)

If ever there was a time we needed an outpouring of wisdom, it is now! I personally long for answers to the questions I never thought we'd be asking. In a world that seems upside down, we need to turn again to the Scriptures, the very words that founded our earth.

In Proverbs 8, the voice of wisdom speaks and describes the fear of the Lord as hatred of evil: "The fear of the LORD is hatred of evil. Pride and arrogance and the way of evil and perverted speech I hate" (v. 13).

Psalm 34 says:

> Come, O children, listen to me;
>   I will teach you the fear of the LORD.
> What man is there who desires life
>   and loves many days, that he may see good?
> Keep your tongue from evil
>   and your lips from speaking deceit.
> Turn away from evil and do good;
>   seek peace and pursue it. (vv. 11–14)

These passages highlight how the combination of perverse speech and prideful ways brings forth evil.

In the book of Job, the fear of the Lord is paired with wisdom: "Behold, the fear of the LORD, that is wisdom, and to turn away from evil is understanding" (28:28).

Other passages describe the fear of the Lord as trembling at his Word. I believe it is also a posture of humility in which we throw ourselves on the mercy of God at the revelation of his holiness and our lack thereof.

Even Jesus took joy in the fear of the Lord. Isaiah prophesied just how the Spirit of God would be seen in the life of Jesus:

> And the Spirit of the LORD shall rest upon him, the Spirit of wisdom and understanding, the Spirit of counsel and might, the Spirit of knowledge and the fear of the LORD. And his delight shall be in the fear of the LORD. He shall not judge by what his eyes see, or decide disputes by what his ears hear. (11:2–3)

If we acknowledge the perversity of our ways and thoughts, he does not deal with us according to our base behavior. He does not measure us by our lack but by the height of his adamant love for us.

Evil

Let love be genuine. Abhor what is evil; hold fast to what is good. (Rom. 12:9)

Loving and abhorring are both conscious choices. Loving everyone is hard, but with God it is possible. Loving everything is disingenuous and actually impossible. In our day, evil is unavoidable. I get that. But this doesn't mean we allow ourselves to be overwhelmed and intimidated into silence. This is not the time for neutrality.

We should abhor poverty while loving the impoverished.

We should hate war but love the widows and orphans and refugees it creates.

Hating evil isn't permission to be hateful. We are not terrorists . . . we are Christians. We are those who are anointed to overcome evil with good. So we do not lie and call evil good. We do not argue with words alone. We live truth, speak truth, and contend for truth with the way we live.

The church has not always done this well.

I have not done this well. I want to do this better.

For too long, we have been known for what we are against rather than what and even whom (Jesus) we are for. In an effort to tip the scale back into balance, the church seems to have adopted the world's trend of endorsing *everything* and calling it love. Again, we love *everyone*. But let's do so with the awareness that we are in the midst of a battle, which means we cannot love *everything*. As Charles Spurgeon wrote, "We are bound to love our enemies, but we are not bound to love God's enemies. We are to wish them, as enemies, a complete overthrow, but to wish them as men, a gracious conversion, that they may obtain God's pardon and become his friends, followers and servants."[3]

Move forward in truth, humility, and love and build what could be.

We are so afraid of being accused of being judgmental that we have gone mute. We cannot be like that wife who, after mishandling her first disagreement with her husband, resigns herself to silence rather than to a commitment to learning to do it well. The silence of this wife will ultimately damage their relationship and compromise its growth. Rather than resign ourselves to the failures of the past, let's move forward in truth, humility, and love and build what could be. We begin by committing to abhor our own sympathies toward the things God hates.

As we begin to live the truth in love, others will be able to hear us as we speak the truth in love. This is vital because . . .

Love without truth is a lie.

What Do You Hate?

What you hate is probably something that frightens you. I am not a fan of snakes, spiders, or scorpions. I hate all three, but the worst are snakes. If I see a scorpion, I kill it. I became their sworn enemy when one stung my youngest son when he was four. (Warning: they pretend to be dead so they can sting you.) Spiders are a bit harder for me. The way they move freaks me out. I ask John or one of my sons to kill them. If no men are home, I take them on. Snakes are another story. You can't kill a snake with a shoe. At least I don't think so, but then again, I've never tried.

I write in a corner of our basement. On top of the hutch over my desk is a machete. Without scaring myself too much, I've decided that if I am alone and discover a snake in our house . . . I will attack. I will take blade in hand and, with a loud prayer in my mouth, kill it! I am committed to go for it because a snake cannot be allowed to roam my home and lay eggs. Why? Because people I love are in my house.

There are other things I hate. Things that threaten us all. I hate child sexual abuse. I hate sex trafficking of anyone of any age or gender. And I have never spoken to anyone who is not outraged by both of these. We know that these practices unmake both the victims and the predators. The cruelty and the perversion of them wound and fracture all those involved to their deepest core. Because we love people, it makes sense that we would hate the practice of both of these. But it is not enough to hate sex trafficking and sexual abuse. We must also hate pornography.

Why?

Pornography is the catalyst behind sexual abuse and sex trafficking. We cannot love, like, or even smile at pornography and truly hate sexual abuse and sex trafficking. To truly love the victims of abuse and trafficking, we must abhor the catalyst of abuse and trafficking . . . porn. To love well, we must hate what twists the souls of others into abusing and trapping children and women.

Porn debases love, unmakes intimacy, and degrades God's good and wondrous gift of sex. It enslaves those God longs to set free. Knowing this, I have chosen to despise every form pornography may adopt (literature, movies, print, or online).

I must abhor what pornography does to love because what it does to love is evil. I abhor what pornography does to marriage. I've heard far too many stories of women who lie in bed wondering why their husbands will not touch them. They see themselves as *less* than desirable. If only they were *more* attractive, their husbands would want them. Then they learn they have a rival, a phantom of virtual sex who has corrupted their intimacy. Their husbands have already given their passion to someone online they don't have to touch.

Sadly, more and more women are becoming entrapped in the same cycle of destruction. A recent survey said that one out of three women watch porn on a weekly basis.[4] The *Huffington Post* claimed, "Porn sites get more visitors each month than Netflix, Amazon, and Twitter combined."[5] According to Fight the New Drug, "Last year alone, 91,980,225,000 videos were watched on Pornhub. That's 12.5 videos for every person on the planet."[6]

Yikes!

Porn is not love. Pornography rapes our minds as it objectifies and debases humans created in the beauty and likeness of their Creator. Then shame comes in and overwhelms the ones the imagery has taken captive. We must love the captives while hating the industry that slowly and surely entraps them.

When we do not hate what is evil, our love is not genuine.

The Passion Translation of Romans 12:9 is a bit more poetic:

> Let the inner movement of your heart always be to love one another, and never play the role of an actor wearing a mask. Despise evil and embrace everything that is good and virtuous.

The temptation to be quiet can be overwhelming, especially when we know that speaking out means we will be called ignorant and extreme. Whenever I have spoken out against this issue, I've been attacked by Christians who argue that what they do in private is their own business, and they are correct. But at the same time, I cannot remain silent, because I have seen the other side of pornography. I have seen its victims, who range from trafficked and sexually abused children to shattered marriages and sexual addicts. When I speak out, my social media is hacked and I am inundated with images and pornographic videos by perpetrators.

> When we do not hate what is evil, our love is not genuine.

We can no longer smile at evil from a safe distance. We can't let it catch our eye or allow ourselves to linger in its presence. We cannot be quiet because we don't want to cause trouble. If we are trapped, we need to ask for help. When it comes to protecting love, we cannot be silent. We cannot wear a mask of acceptance.

Following Jesus, Our Example

Charles Spurgeon said, "What Jesus loves, we love; what Jesus hates, we hate; what Jesus seeks, we seek; what Jesus shuns, we shun. This is true friendship when there is but one heart in two bodies."[7]

As Spurgeon said, Jesus is our example in both love and hate. What does Jesus love? People. Jesus loves and seeks the rescue of all lost people. Jesus loved his enemies and called them friends. Friendship with God does not include hating people.

What does Jesus hate? Jesus hates the enemies of love . . . hypocritical religion being one of the first and foremost. As I probed the meaning of hypocrisy, I saw areas where I am hypocritical. Where I wanted relationships with people more than I wanted their rescue. Where I was silent rather than loving. Where I flirted from afar rather than turning quickly away. What I refuse to abhor now will become normal in the lives of my grandchildren.

G. K. Chesterton said, "Tolerance is the virtue of a man without convictions." I fear we've chosen to tolerate things that will one day threaten to overwhelm us. We must always be kind and respectful, but the silence of tolerance can quickly morph into endorsement.

What does Jesus seek? Jesus told us: "But seek first the kingdom of God and his righteousness, and all these things will be added to you" (Matt. 6:33).

What does it mean to shun, and what does Jesus shun? *Shun* means to avoid something by turning away from it. It is actually what we have already described. We don't sit with evil, wink at perversity, or converse about vain things. Paul describes it well:

> To open their eyes, so that they may turn from darkness to light and from the power of Satan to God, that they may receive forgiveness of sins and a place among those who are sanctified by faith in me. (Acts 26:18)

We don't turn from people. We pray they turn from what shadows their souls.

Before I was born again, I was an enemy of Christ rather than his friend. When my hardened heart became a heart of flesh, I felt what pained his heart. Following the lead of Jesus is a lifestyle. We turn from what we used to hold dear to lay hold of what he treasures.

More than a century ago, Charles Spurgeon wrote, "The present age is so flippant that if a man loves the savior he is a fanatic and if he hates the powers of evil he is a bigot."[8]

I cannot even imagine what he would say of our day. Our culture is no longer flippant—it is depraved.

We *must* love the truth that sets people free while hating the lies that bind them.

Just as God is light without darkness, he is good without evil. An all-good God cannot be part bad. There is no alliance between light and dark, no partnership between right and wrong, and demon idols do not belong in God's temple. And what of Jesus? The book of Hebrews quotes the prophecy of David in Psalm 45:6–7:

> But of the Son he says, "Your throne, O God, is forever and ever, the scepter of uprightness is the scepter of your kingdom. You have loved righteousness and hated wickedness; therefore God, your God, has anointed you with the oil of gladness beyond your companions." (Heb. 1:8–9)

Jesus loves righteousness and hates wickedness. Can we his disciples do any different? It is time we remembered that persecution is part of the package.

> Blessed are you when people hate you and when they exclude you and revile you and spurn your name as evil, on account of the Son of Man! Rejoice in that day, and leap for joy, for behold, your reward is great in heaven; for so their fathers did to the prophets. (Luke 6:22–23)

Discernment

Charles Spurgeon said, "Discernment is not knowing the difference between right and wrong, it is knowing the difference between right and almost right."[9]

There is so much that sounds right and feels wrong. We are in days that require a thorough knowledge of the Scriptures coupled with the leading of the Holy Spirit. Scripture will give us the framework and the Spirit of the Most High God will give us the words of life. We need the Holy Spirit to illuminate the Word of God so that we can know how to love the who and how to hate the what. To that end, I

137

leaned heavily on Scripture as I wrote this chapter. There were actually far too many passages to cover in these pages, so I included more for your reference in appendix 1. Please pray and ask the Holy Spirit how these passages should be applied in your personal life. Rather than tell you what to think, I want to allow the Holy Spirit to lead you. As we move into this next chapter, will you pray with me?

Dear heavenly Father,
I want to love what and how you love. I don't want to be a hypocrite. I don't want to act in arrogance. I ask you to teach me what you hate so that your love would flourish in my life. Holy Spirit, breathe on these Scripture passages and personalize them for me. Give me the courage to break the silence with words that set the captives free. In Jesus's name, amen.

7

ADAMANT FOR TRUTH

> Where I found truth, there found I my God, who
> is truth itself.
>
> St. Augustine

Even though we've all lied, the pursuit of truth is woven deep within us. Without truth, we are like ships without rudders, driven by every wind of doctrine and whim of emotion, which cannot help but drive us to the brink of destruction. As we pursue truth, it will have its way with us. Truth is not a "what," it is a "who."

Rather than argue about what is true, we must remember why truth is important. And once we remember, truth must be lived because the truth is alive. We live truth as we lift our souls to our Lord and Savior, who told us, "I am the way, and the truth, and the life. No one comes to the Father except through me" (John 14:6).

For this statement to be true, each element must stand on its own. If Jesus is *the* way and not merely one of *many* ways, then it must be true that no one comes to the Father except through him. If Jesus lied and misrepresented who he was and he is but one of many ways to the Father, then he cannot be the truth. If he is not the truth, it is impossible for Jesus to be the life.

Jesus is absolutely *all* that he says he is or absolutely *none* of it. It is impossible for him to be both. In the words of Benjamin Franklin, "Half a truth is often a great lie." Every partial truth is seeded with a lie. If Jesus is in fact the way, he must also be the truth and the life.

> **Jesus is absolutely *all* that he says he is or absolutely *none* of it.**

But our culture pushes back on absolutes. We've been led to believe they are too confining and harsh. The truth cannot help but exclude lies, but it does so in a manner that is at once immovable and gentle. Truth should be soft in the telling and implacable and absolute in principle.

Absolutes are foundational. And foundations are unmovable. As such absolutes are not harsh or restrictive—they are protective. Without absolutes, which are unchanging truths, we are doomed to build on sand. Absolutes are the principles that protect us and the convictions that anchor us when the storms of life hit or temptations lure.

All Roads Do Not Lead to Rome

In ancient times, people said, "All roads lead to Rome," because at the time Rome was the hub of the Roman road system. But as time marched on and the Roman Empire fell from its lofty height of power, this saying was no longer true. It became a figure of speech that means all paths eventually lead to the same place. What was once true of Rome cannot be applied to the kingdom of God.

God's truth does not shift and morph as the balance of human power and thought changes. Truth is more than timeless . . . it is eternal. The road to God begins at the door: Jesus Christ. Why would God send his only begotten Son if there were other options? Why send Jesus if he was just the best option? I wouldn't volunteer any of my sons—unless it was the only way. Jesus alone is our atonement. It is a grave mistake to believe that all roads lead to salvation, even though all roads lead to an encounter with Jesus. Scripture tells us:

> Therefore God has highly exalted him and bestowed on him the name that is above every name, so that at the name of Jesus every knee should bow, in heaven and on earth and under the earth, and every tongue confess that Jesus Christ is Lord, to the glory of God the Father. (Phil. 2:9–11)

"Those under the earth" speaks of the demonic realm. The day will come when they will have to acknowledge Jesus's supremacy, even though they won't experience Jesus as Savior.

Perhaps you might reason that all truth is relative and there is no reason to be this extreme. Perhaps you believe that what is truth for me may not be truth for you.

If this is in your mind, then we are not talking about the same thing. When I speak of absolute truth, I'm not talking about things that could be true *of* me but not *of* you. For example, I'm half Sicilian. I'm married. I'm a mother and a grandmother. All these aspects are true of me now, but they are not true of everyone. Therefore, they are not the truth; they are just true. Conversely, what was true about me ten years ago may not necessarily be true about me today.

Another example of something being true and yet not the truth is that outside my window the sky is a pristine Colorado blue. I can confidently declare, "The sky is blue!" and for the next few hours my words will hold true. But they are not the truth, for they break the parameter that truth must be consistent. When the sun sets, the sky will no longer be blue. Therefore, what was true at noon will not be true at midnight. In far too many ways, I fear we are in the midnight of our human souls.

"True of" describes attributes, seasons, and aspects of our lives. What was true in one season is not necessarily true in the next. These kinds of truths live in the domain of our particular worlds and are subject to change. Anything that applies only to some cannot ultimately be the truth. True can be relative; the truth is never relative.

If we are not careful with truth, it will become a casualty in our current culture. This is why we all need to know the ancient texts, so we can discern truth independent of the sway of public opinion and our own feelings about a matter. When truth is tied to perspective, it is called *relativism*. Relativism is the belief that different things are true, right, etc., for different people or at different times. Under this definition, truth would vary constantly.

The ideology of relativism undermines the very meaning of truth. For something to be truth, it must be true at all times. If this weren't so, then someone could lie and say that something was *their truth*. Perception cannot be allowed to determine truth. If it did, we would all be seeing through a different lens. We need an immovable Adamant who anchors our souls to the perspective of our Creator.

As Christians, we cannot believe the truth is relative, because we believe the Truth is our relative, Jesus Christ, our brother, Cornerstone, Lord, and Adamant. God's Word (Jesus) transforms us, while relativism conforms us.

Being the truth is a very different matter than telling the truth or even describing yourself accurately. Even if it were possible for any of us to be completely truthful, we could never *be* the truth.

We can tell truth.

We can live truth.

We can love truth.

We can hate truth.

We can deny truth.

We can believe truth.

But only Christ can claim to *be* the truth.

Buddha had many true sayings, but he did not claim to *be* the truth. Buddha acknowledged he was a man in pursuit of truth. Likewise, Muhammad said many things that were true, but he did not claim to *be* the truth.

Jesus didn't say, "I pursue truth" or "I am one of many truths." He said, "I am the truth." And when we say all roads lead to Rome (salvation), we call Jesus a liar.

What Is Truth?

What is truth after all? Since the beginning of time, humankind has posed this question. We find our answer in Jesus's words in the Gospel of John: "Sanctify them in the truth; your word is truth" (17:17).

This verse doesn't say the Word has truth in it, which of course it does, but that God's Word *is* truth. Jesus is the Word made flesh, so his life expresses what living truth looks like.

143

The truth blesses and consecrates us so that we are set apart for his holy purpose. Outside of Jesus, who is truth, there can be no holiness. If God's Word is truth and Jesus is the Word made flesh, then Jesus is the truth. Ultimately, truth is not subjective; yet one day we will all be subject to truth.

> Every word of God proves true;
>   he is a shield to those who take refuge in him.
> Do not add to his words,
>   lest he rebuke you and you be found a liar.
>   (Prov. 30:5–6)

Many believe we have advanced in wisdom and evolved into higher forms of reasoning and it is time to reinterpret the Scriptures. How can we imagine this when there is global upheaval? Each day we hear of another act of cruelty.

If we're the measure of wisdom, then it would seem the earth has weighed us and found us wanting. Rather than imagine ourselves enlightened, we need to ask for God's light.

> Send out your light and your truth;
>   let them lead me;
> let them bring me to your holy hill
>   and to your dwelling! (Ps. 43:3)

Light and truth are faithful guides. God is light, the source of all truth. Light illuminates and truth stands. Truth could be likened to markers and signposts, and light is how we find our way. But when markers are moved, people can easily lose their way.

> Enter by the narrow gate. For the gate is wide and the way is easy that leads to destruction, and those who enter by it

are many. For the gate is narrow and the way is hard that leads to life, and those who find it are few. (Matt. 7:13–14)

Jesus is the narrow gate that leads to life. The way is certain but hard. It has been argued that a loving God would include everyone. He did. He invites all to *come*. The way was made, but we are left to choose which path we will take. Jesus will not force us through the narrow gate. He will not lie about the cost of following. He will not say it is easy when it's not. He has gone before us and invites us to follow: "If you would be my disciples deny yourself, take up your cross and follow" (see Mark 8:34).

Matthew 7:13 mentions another gate. It has a wide entrance leading to a broad and easy path. The words on its entry encourage us to live for ourselves, to follow our dreams. The broad entrance allows us to carry with us as much as we'd like. It is a much more popular gate that leads to destruction.

In this realm, we only see as though peering through a darkened mirror, which is why we need light and truth to be our companions as we pursue the high and holy life God has called us to. Light dispels the darkness that comes when we live in the shadowed realm of our own understanding.

The fact that the truth might be inconvenient or unpopular does not change the fact that it is truth. Truth is eternal, woven in the Word and statutes of the Most High God. Truth does not subject itself to an opinion poll or a popularity contest.

Truthful Can Be Tricky

We have all lied. Some of us have lied thinking we were telling the truth. At other times, we knew what we were doing and just plain lied. We have all been lied to. Just as we have lied unwittingly, others have lied to us unintentionally, thinking they were telling us the truth. And there were times that lies were told intentionally. Not only have we all lied and been lied to, but we also have all believed lies. Okay, I will just make this personal. *I've* believed lies.

There are many reasons for lying. Lies are told to protect people from being hurt. People lie when they are afraid. Lies are told to prevent loss. People lie when they don't want to lose a relationship, possession, or position. Lies can also be told to gain these things.

Lies spread until the truth is told.

You were created for truth. So no matter how frightening it may be at the time, we must always be truthful with ourselves. Lying to ourselves makes us feel ill at ease. There are areas in my life that I lied to myself about for years. But we must remember that the truth will keep us in the end.

Not only have I embraced falsehoods about myself, but I have also listened to lies about others. I can't even begin to number the times I was absolutely certain that something was true only to find out later that I was wrong.

If I am left to my own devices, my capacity to reason can range from logical and well thought out to emotional and utterly ridiculous. My feelings have kidnapped my sense of discernment more times than I'd like to admit and held it hostage to the dictates of a lie. Until a lie is brought out of hiding and examined by the light of truth, it will grow unchecked. Lies spread until the truth is told.

Living in Truth

> So Jesus said to the Jews who had believed him, "If you abide in my word, you are truly my disciples, and you will know the truth, and the truth will set you free." (John 8:31–32)

As we live in the truth (God's Word), we will come to intimately know the truth, and the truth that we live will set us free. Living in truth breaks the bonds of captivity just as surely as living in lies binds us. Jesus invites us to truth, just as all were invited to the wedding feast.

> "Go therefore to the main roads and invite to the wedding feast as many as you find." And those servants went out into the roads and gathered all whom they found, both bad and good. So the wedding hall was filled with guests.
> But when the king came in to look at the guests, he saw there a man who had no wedding garment. And he said to him, "Friend, how did you get in here without a wedding garment?" And he was speechless. Then the king said to the attendants, "Bind him hand and foot and cast him into the outer darkness. In that place there will be weeping and gnashing of teeth." For many are called, but few are chosen. (Matt. 22:9–14)

Everyone is invited to live in truth, but there is a dress code. We come clothed in Christ and his righteousness, not our own filthy rags. The Lamb is our wedding garment, our adamant way and covering Cornerstone.

The truth can be offensive. Thomas Paine said, "He who dares not offend cannot be honest." I would rather be offended by the truth than enter into eternity by way of a lie. Likewise, I would rather risk offending people than lie.

Jesus offended his very closest disciples. In the Gospel of John, we read:

> Many of his disciples said, "This is very hard to understand. How can anyone accept it?" Jesus was aware that his disciples were complaining, so he said to them, "Does this offend you?" (6:60–61 NLT)

Why were they offended? Well, Jesus had just dropped a pretty intense truth bomb. A few verses earlier he had declared, "I tell you the truth, unless you eat the flesh of the Son of Man and drink his blood, you cannot have eternal life within you" (6:53 NLT).

Okay. This was way outside their frame of reference. Jesus knew his words wouldn't make sense to them in the moment. He also knew they would make complete sense to them later. I guess the question we must all ask ourselves is, Will we follow Jesus (truth) even when we don't understand?

This question needs to be answered on so many levels. We must answer it as parents, friends, spouses, leaders, consumers, and, most importantly, servants of the living God.

Will we follow Jesus (truth) even when we don't understand?

For example, if I am in a relationship that is unhealthy and I never address it, then I'm enabling unhealthy behavior. It's not Christian to be quiet; it's confusing. We all have a chance to grow when there are healthy confrontations and conversations. If nothing is said and the dynamic continues, resentment will build up and suddenly there will be a breach that the other person never saw coming. We rarely have a good outcome with bad input. And the same is true of no input.

If something isn't addressed, it's endorsed. When we don't address things, we are saying, "I don't care enough about you or our relationship to build for our future." When we care, we share. We say things in a way that they can be heard in order to construct proper channels of communication for the future. If we truly care about the body of Christ, we need to be careful that our actions and inactions, words and silence always honor truth.

Living with Courage and Conviction

As God puts his hand on us, it is evidenced in our lives. When the Word of God is not only preached with boldness but also lived with confidence, there is an atmosphere for change. There is a shift. We don't just hear truth . . . we live truth. As the Holy Spirit quickens us, we come to attention, stand straighter, and have a greater awareness that the truth we carry within us is sacred. When God's Word is preached through our lives, the Holy Spirit puts steel in our convictions.

Those who have ears to hear will likewise receive the wisdom and courage to live in truth. The Word of God falls on good soil and produces a harvest first and foremost in our lives. This happens first *in* us so it can happen next *through* us.

Recently, I had a text conversation with a beautiful, young, brave daughter in the faith. She asked me how I reconciled the fact that public people with amazing spiritual gifts had personal lives that were in shambles. Their private lives were plagued with everything from adultery, alcohol abuse, to a lack of financial transparency. I explained that I believe our lives preach louder than our gifts. God's gifts are meant to be surrounded by the fruit of the Spirit, which is cultivated when we allow truth to have its way.

When we know the truth, we cannot act as though we are ignorant of it. If we don't know the truth, we are invited to seek it. We seek it in God's Word and see it in the life of Jesus. And once it's discovered, we cannot continue to close our ears to the deafening cry for truth in a culture captive to the lies it told itself. Even now people are discovering that what they thought was freedom is in fact chains. Jesus is our truth in a world of lies.

Truth is both lion and lamb.

Truth is adamant, impervious to lies, and unmoved by the river of time.

Truth speaks as loud in a whisper as it does in a shout.

Truth is neither strengthened nor diminished by opinion.

Truth is hard but never harsh.

Truth does not argue, because it is the final word.

Truth is more than timeless; it is eternal.

Truth breeds conviction.

We adamantly oppose any degradation of the truth by living the Word of truth. Truth should be evident in our personal lives. We cannot choose to remain in a posture of quiet comfort when so many are living in the discomfort of lies.

Dear heavenly Father,
May your truth be evident in my life. I ask you to give
me strength to live in the courage of my convictions,
to speak your truth, and to live your truth. May my
words be tender and never harsh. May every aspect of
my life express your truth in love.

8

ADAMANT IN WORD

When you have thrown a stone, you cannot afterwards bring it back again, but nevertheless you are responsible for having taken up the stone and flung it, for the origin of the act was within you.

Aristotle

Our words create sound waves that act like so many far-flung stones in an ocean called the world. As our access to the hearts and ears of others increases, so does our need for accountability and wisdom.

Recently, I heard there is a giant trash vortex out in the Pacific. Some accounts say it is larger than Mexico; another source says it dwarfs the state of Texas. This particular one is referred to as the "North Pacific Garbage Patch." It spans up to a million square miles and measures as much as 8.3 billion metric tons. This mass of plastic floats in the ocean, caught up in and thrown together by the ocean currents. Plastic can take up to four hundred years to degrade, so there is a very real concern that the amount of plastic in the ocean could supersede the total weight of sea life by the year 2050. As the plastic breaks into smaller pieces, it is consumed by seagulls and various other forms of marine life. The plastic particles eventually find their way into fish, which are eaten by humans. In addition to killing marine life and potentially poisoning humans, this biohazard could one day make navigating the ocean difficult. My point is that plastic never truly goes away, and as time passes, the particles become increasingly unrecognizable and dangerous.[1]

I couldn't help but draw a parallel between this epic amount of plastic waste and our wasteful, harmful, polluting words. Leonardo da Vinci echoed the insight of Aristotle:

> If you throw a stone in a pond . . . the waves, which strike against the shores are thrown back towards the spot where the stone struck; and on meeting other waves they never intercept each other's course. . . . In a small pond one and the same stroke gives birth to many motions of advance and recoil.[2]

Advance and recoil. Are our words advancing the cause of Christ or causing others to recoil? If only our stones were isolated to small ponds! But alas, they drop and make waves in a universe of water. We live in a day when no matter how far away we cast a stone, its impact will come back to be felt on our shores. If what we communicate is our conviction of the love of God, bands of goodness will be set in motion. But if we cast stones of gossip and slander, then the waves that return to us will be of the same kind.

Words are a sacred entrustment from the Creator. No one has the right to cast whatever they might feel at any given moment into the ocean of opinions and then make others responsible for sorting through poorly chosen messaging. Doing so is really no different than littering. Once our words are out there . . . they are out there. We are responsible for what we do with our words. This includes what we write, speak, post, and repost. Grace did not eliminate the warnings of the New Testament. Listen to James:

> Not many of you should become teachers, my brothers, for you know that we who teach will be judged with greater strictness. (James 3:1)

Teaching includes imparting, communicating, explaining, showing, instructing, educating, clarifying, and demonstrating. This verse is not reserved solely for teachers. If we do any of these things, the warning applies to us. Posting on social media, blogging, and teaching in our local churches should be done in a spirit of truth, wisdom, and relational and theological accountability. Everything we write, teach, and say must be in keeping with the counsel of Scripture.

Opinion versus Conviction?

Being adamant in word requires the ability to discern between opinion and truth. Opinions are so easy to form and so hard to keep to ourselves. If we are not careful, the giving and receiving of opinions can become addictive. We have at our fingertips access to what everyone thinks and feels. At the same

Opinions are so easy to form and so hard to keep to ourselves.

153

time, we have the ability to put any opinion we may hold out into the opinion ocean in seconds. It can be exciting to hear what everyone is saying, especially when they talk to us. But here is where I must warn you: don't give the opinions of relative strangers too much power over you.

Don't let strangers wound you with the arrows of their careless words. Don't grant your virtual community more access to you than your real one. You were born to scale mountains, not merely scan phones. You were born for face-to-face connection, not emojis. Speak God's Word rather than merely echo it in likes and reposts. None of these things are wrong, but they are far from enough. You were made for involvement.

Don't get entrapped in comparison when deep down you are hungry for something more. You were wired for your Creator. Why listen to strangers when you have been invited into an intimate conversation with the Most High? God has invited you to come into his very presence. It is there, free from comparison and distraction, that the Holy Spirit will breathe life into you and stand you on your feet and fill your mouth with his Word. Make room in your life for God's Spirit.

We live in a day when there are more opinions than convictions, which is rough. Opinions pull and push at us, while convictions ground us. Convictions are attached to belief systems. Opinions are free-flowing, like so many plastic bottles floating in the ocean. Opinions are about something or someone and trend with what is happening in the culture. As Christians, we should have convictions that are shaped by Scripture, and these convictions should shape our opinions. Don't allow opinions to uproot your convictions.

Resolute

> Keep your eyes open, hold tight to your convictions, give it
> all you've got, be resolute. (1 Cor. 16:13 Message)

What does it mean to be resolute? It means adamant. Immovable, uncompromising, and invincible.

As an extraverted, intuitive, feeling, and perceiving personality type, commonly known as an ENFP, this is a challenge for me. My default is to put my feelings and everyone else's in the driver's seat of my life. I want everyone to be right, feel right, be happy, be heard, and be included. At the same time, I can be highly opinionated and fiercely passionate about everything ranging from my morning espresso to social justice issues. (Yes, it is exhausting!) I'd go rogue if it weren't for the Word of God. Without it, I would be like a kite without a tail, soaring one moment and crashing the next. I must intentionally decide that my opinions will be subjected to my convictions. If they are not, any whim of popular culture can waylay me.

Social media can magnify both our weaknesses and our strengths. Years ago, I got entangled in a back-and-forth on Facebook. I was working under the impression that maybe I wasn't explaining myself well enough and if I could just be clearer, then the light would go on for those who were arguing with me. I wasn't getting anywhere because unknowingly I had engaged in an argument with a troll. (I told you they were real!)

I stopped only because one of my sons happened to observe the interchange, grabbed his phone, and explained, "Mom, they don't want to understand. They want to fight you in front of a large audience. They are using your platform to attack you. Stop talking to them! Just block them."

I wondered if I could block someone. Wouldn't that be mean? No—in this case, it was a move to protect my platform and the people who visited it. There is a vast difference between social media and hostile media.

This was a revelation to say the least.

What we were discussing wasn't an issue of eternal importance. It was a matter of opinion rather than a core conviction. We have all seen a social media crowd go mob on an individual or an issue . . . fast. As a result, I've learned to have strong convictions and gentle opinions.

Social media is definitely one of the areas where the mob challenge is the greatest. You have permission to post and go. Use your gift of words to bless, strengthen, encourage, and guide. Follow people who do the same. Affirm what merits affirmation, interact with what is healthy, ask questions respectfully, but live to please God, not people. We have been forewarned in Scripture:

> But you need to *be aware* that in the final days the culture
> of society will sink so low into degradation that it will be
> extremely difficult for the people of God. (2 Tim. 3:1 TPT)

In the King James Version, this verse reads, "This know also" and describes the times as "perilous." The English Standard Version admonishes us, "Understand this . . . there will come times of difficulty." The Message says, "Don't be naive. There are difficult times ahead."

As far as I am concerned, the difficulty has begun. Degradation always begins with a systematic undermining of structure and truth. As we become adamant in the truth of Jesus as the way, let's also learn to be adamant in word based on our convictions. Let's take Paul's message to the early church as our own:

> For we know, brothers loved by God, that he has chosen you, because our gospel came to you not only in word, but also in power and in the Holy Spirit and with full conviction. You know what kind of men we proved to be among you for your sake. And you became imitators of us and of the Lord, for you received the word in much affliction, with the joy of the Holy Spirit. (1 Thess. 1:4–6)

It's time we listened to—and dare I say obeyed—the One who gave us the privilege of words. The very One who confused the languages so long ago at the tower of Babel could have silenced us, but instead he chose to instruct us in his gift of speech.

When I was writing *Without Rival*, I was working on a chapter that covered a topic I cannot feel neutral about: gender. In my rough draft, I systematically confronted the distortions of another leader, convinced I needed to leave no stone unturned. My prose became a lot of back-and-forth until I realized I was lost in the forest of opinions, so I sent the chapter to one of my trusted friends.

She very lovingly told me that my words had morphed into a rant. Somewhere along the line I had gone from writing to venting, and by doing so, I was pulling my audience into strife. She pointed out what section

> As we become adamant in the truth of Jesus as the way, let's also learn to be adamant in word based on our convictions.

should be eliminated . . . it was half the chapter. I listened. I edited. I'm glad I did. None of us can risk being adrift in the universe of opinions. We all need people in our lives who will tell us what we don't want to hear. These are people we have a real relationship with. People who are accessible and have our cell phone numbers. People we are submitted to. Yes, I said it. If we are not under authority, then we do not truly have authority. A certain number of followers does not grant any of us authority. A close-knit circle of accountability does.

> We all need people in our lives who will tell us what we don't want to hear.

We live in a culture where opinions fly unchecked and words are launched like missiles at both strangers and friends. This is all in direct opposition to the admonishment found in the book of James (be quick to hear, slow to speak, and slow to anger [1:19]). People often allow their words to take wing without realizing what they have loosed upon an unsuspecting world. In this time of easy access and low accountability, we really have no way of knowing the reach of our words or the measure of their effect. We cannot contain what we cannot measure.

I stay away from certain forums because Scripture warns us, "Have nothing to do with foolish, ignorant controversies; you know that they breed quarrels" (2 Tim. 2:23). If I don't have all the information, I don't need to weigh in on the matter. If I'm not responsible, do I really need to respond? My opinions may ebb and flow according to my feelings about something or someone. I try (as much as possible) not to allow my opinions about something to override my convictions.

To be propelled by truth and not opinion, we must be acquainted with the truth found in Scripture, and sometimes we need help to discern it. A friend of mine was sharing how she was reading some things that just felt off to her, but she was already emotionally involved with the writing of the author, so she brought it to her husband. He went through it line by line and pointed out where the writing had changed from biblical truth to the author's experience. Even the apostle Paul confronted Peter when he saw Peter living one way among the Gentiles and another among the Jews. We all need truth tellers.

The Power of Words

Words are seeds that can produce life or death. Words are stones that can build or kill. Let's not say we love Scripture and then contradict it with our words. Words are precious— and dangerous.

In the Middle East, stoning was and is a form of capital punishment that was adopted so that no one person could be blamed for the death of the guilty. Stoning happens in our Western world as well. It is just that we practice a different sort of stoning. We don't throw rocks . . . we hurl words. And the more people who take part in the word toss, the less guilty we feel. If everyone is saying something, then no one is guilty, right?

Our culture may affirm this type of reasoning, but we cannot. We answer to a higher purpose and standard. We are not citizens of this world. We are ambassadors of an eternal kingdom. We understand the power of words even if this earth does not. We cannot afford to stone others, because we know better, and those who know better are empowered to do better.

The lamp of God's Word and the leading of his Spirit are essential if we are to navigate this universe of opinions. Lies escalate under the cover of confusion. I don't have all the answers, and it would be impossible for me to speak into your unique situation. I don't want to tell you how to act; I should point you to the source and position you to listen and learn.

Gossip

Let's be mindful of what we say and stop grieving God. Gossip has never glorified God, and at times, gossip is all social media is. The first time I grieved the Spirit of God I sensed it immediately. No one had to tell me. I knew. I don't remember what I said. I remember what I felt. Suddenly, there was a disruptive flutter within my stomach . . . almost a presentiment of alarm warning of impending danger.

It was similar to the feeling I experienced as a child when I lied to my parents. It had been years since I had felt that. In fact, I'd spent the last decade saying whatever I wanted. It hadn't bothered me before when I'd said something about someone in less than flattering terms. Wasn't I just repeating what I had seen or heard? Why was I feeling this when all my sins were forgiven?

What I didn't understand at the beginning of my Christian walk was that everything had changed when I invited the Holy Spirit to counsel me in all things. He takes this job seriously!

Most of us would never intentionally rob, murder, or curse another person, but gossip can make us guilty of doing all three. I know my mouth has caused me more trouble than anything else in my life. Sadly, what I have spoken has caused other people trouble as well. I've troubled the heart of my husband with careless words more times than I'd like to admit. I've troubled my children with words too weak or too strong. I've spoken against things I didn't have any right to raise my voice about. I've been quiet when I should have reached out. I also know other people's words have caused me more problems than I thought possible.

Words That Heal

Words can be one of the most constructive and one of the most destructive forces on the planet. Yet just as surely as I have been wounded by the words of people, the Word of God has healed me. This has happened as others have spoken the truth of God's Word into and over my life. It has happened in my times of devotion or prayer when a passage or a verse has suddenly arrested me. In a moment's time, everything shifts and my eyes are opened. When we listen to and believe the wisdom of our Creator, we have the chance to learn the right thing the easy way.

> Religion that is pure and undefiled before God the Father is this: to visit orphans and widows in their affliction, and to keep oneself unstained from the world. (James 1:27)

We love this verse. But how often do we hear the words of the previous verse quoted?

If anyone thinks he is religious and does not bridle his tongue but deceives his heart, this person's religion is worthless. (James 1:26)

Rogue Words

Don't risk staining what you do with what you say. James is telling us that if we do right while saying wrong, our religion is deceptive and worthless. Why? Because nothing reveals the condition of our hearts more than what we say.

Sorry, friends. We have work to do.

The book of James goes on to say:

> For we all stumble in many ways. And if anyone does not stumble in what he says, he is a perfect man, able also to bridle his whole body. If we put bits into the mouths of horses so that they obey us, we guide their whole bodies as well. (3:2–3)

> Don't risk staining what you do with what you say.

Jesus was the only perfect man who spoke only what he heard his Father say. James the brother of Jesus uses an interesting choice of imagery here. There is a correlation between the words we speak—or don't speak—and the direction of our lives. Next he moves from traveling roads to navigating the currents of the sea.

> Look at the ships also: though they are so large and are driven by strong winds, they are guided by a very small rudder wherever the will of the pilot directs. (3:4)

Even when the winds are strong and life seems overwhelming, speaking God's Word guides us through the storms of life.

So also the tongue is a small member, yet it boasts of great things. How great a forest is set ablaze by such a small fire! (3:5)

Let's not burn the place down or derail ourselves or our brothers and sisters.

During World War II, the phrase "Loose lips sink ships" was used to remind people of the potential danger posed by unguarded conversations. People needed to be mindful of carelessly giving away information that could be used by covert enemies. In times of war, we can never be certain about who is listening.

Does God want to launch something in your life that you might be sinking with your words? Are you riding that pony in the wrong direction?

Maybe there is a promotion or an opportunity you are hoping for.

Maybe there is a relationship you want to see healed and restored.

Maybe there are prayers that your words and actions are undermining.

Maybe you are talking in a season of listening.

Maybe your tone is wrong.

Maybe you have started the right conversation with the wrong people.

Maybe you are in a season of learning.

Maybe you have more questions than answers.

Matthew 12:36–37 promises us, "You can be sure of this: when the day of judgment comes, everyone will be held accountable for every careless word he has spoken. Your very words will be used as evidence against you, and your words will declare you either innocent or guilty" (TPT).

We are judged by what we say and by how we choose to respond to what Jesus said. I want my words to honor his life. At the end of the day, I want to create disciples, not attract religious tourists.

Right Questions, Wrong Audience

I live with several males, which means it can be difficult to get my hands on the remote control. Recently, we were away on vacation and looking for something we could watch as a family when the man in charge of the remote paused on a scene from *The Godfather*. In deference to my Sicilian roots, I am sharing the quote we heard: "Never tell anybody outside the family what you are thinking."

"Never" probably works only in the realm of mafia, but there is still wisdom to be found here. Healthy families are still the best place to process what we are thinking. There are no perfect families—only healthy ones committed to the growth of all their members.

Perhaps you are thinking, *Wait, Lisa. None of my family members are Christians.* I want you to feel free to think of your family in larger terms. You are welcome to process things within the household of faith. Family is the people who are there for you. They could be the people you worship with, your small group, or even Christian employees who work alongside you. Social media is not family. Social media is great for input but not for processing.

The movie also gave us this line: "Don't ever take sides with anyone against the family again. Ever."

Our family of faith has issues. Does the church need to grow when it comes to empowering women? Yes! Have things gotten better? Yes! Are there other issues to address? Yes! But what do we gain when we take sides against God's bride?

Recently, there was a tweet that invited women to share their grievances with church leadership and how they handle women. It went viral. So many women added their voices to the conversation, and it became a free-for-all. I noticed that if anyone said their experience with the church was good, they were shut down.

Did this conversation need to happen? Yes. But I question whether social media is the right medium for pointing out a problem, even though it is a great one for volunteering a solution.

If you have the answer, declare it from every social media rooftop! But if you want to complain, criticize, or strategize, make sure you have the attention of the right people. Knowing who is at your table is impossible when you are working with social media. Let's talk to the right people about the right questions.

Hosting forums that malign the church on social media or any public forum is akin to exposing the bride when she is believed to be behaving badly. Is this helpful when Scripture tells us there is a world system that already hates us? Does it benefit the people in the valley of decision who have no context for our arguments?

Publicly, we should humble ourselves and acknowledge that we have failed to love well. Then we should rise together and speak to what could be rather than denounce what is.

Too often we're having the right conversation with the wrong people. When we do this, we all look stupid.

Viral

Sometimes when something goes viral online, people are being infected rather than influenced. Let's be careful that our posts make a lasting change rather than a name for the one who posted. Let's be slow to attack how and what others have built. Let's be builders rather than demolishers of the houses of worship. I too have been a victim of all the prejudice leveled at women. I'm nearly sixty years old, and I'm still attacked by some for being seductive or bold. I refuse to stop what I am building to argue with the inane comments of a few. I am anointed to prophesy, not criticize, and to build rather than tear down. And so are you!

> Let's be builders rather than demolishers.

To get the right answer, we need to gather the right people around the table. This means we invite older and younger women of all races into the conversation. When these conversations happen in our real communities, we get the benefit of the questions of the daughters, the answers and experience of the mothers, and the wisdom and perspective of the grandmothers. This is a threefold cord that will not be easily broken.

Measuring Our Words

Social media can be a tool for so much good. We have encouragement at our fingertips. Information can be disseminated quickly. Prayer can be requested for anything ranging from a personal need to a national crisis. Many of you were kind enough to pray for me as I wrote this book. On so many fronts, social media can be helpful, encouraging, challenging, informative, and even educational.

I do not take lightly the privilege or the liability of social media. At times I have made mistakes and failed to measure my words. Having said this, I have also discovered that I can carefully craft words and still be misunderstood. This is because we don't really know whom we are talking to, which is one of the keys to effective communication. Everyone has different filters through which they hear and see.

I try to use social media to minister to those who grant me the honor of access to their lives. Some of my posts are just fun and silly, and others are serious. This is the rhythm of life. On some days I do the social media dance better than on others. I've learned to limit my opinions (even though I certainly have them). As much as possible, I try not to say things that contradict Scripture or how I live. I am silent when I can't say something nice about someone or something. (Not easy.)

One of the best ways to guard our hearts is to guard the words that we allow to enter our lives. There are times when others are less than kind. I am sure you've experienced the fallout from bullies and trolls on social media. In the course of a day, I might be called everything from a mama lioness to a heretical woman who should remain silent. (And those are the nice names.) In all this, I've learned to develop thick skin and a tender heart.

With the vast range of emotion present and available to one and all on social media, I intentionally limit the personal dramas that I allow entrance into my life. In the context of our day, let's revisit the words of 2 Timothy 2:23–26:

Have nothing to do with foolish, ignorant controversies; you know that they breed quarrels. And the Lord's servant must not be quarrelsome but kind to everyone, able to teach, patiently enduring evil, correcting his opponents with gentleness. God may perhaps grant them repentance leading to a knowledge of the truth, and they may come to their senses and escape from the snare of the devil, after being captured by him to do his will.

Not everything or everyone deserves a response. Sometimes an answer validates their foolishness. Not everyone needs to know we've been mistreated. We're bigger than that. We need to take our pain to the high court of our Father rather than the jury of a faceless mob.

Popular or Influential?

Recently, I sensed the Holy Spirit asking me, "Lisa, do you want to be popular or influential?"

I answered, "Influential."

To successfully navigate this opinionated world, we need to regularly ask ourselves this question: popular or influential? Maybe you are reading this book because you know you're called to be an influencer for good. This means at times you will take a stand that is less than popular. To gain a bit more understanding, let's define these terms and highlight their differences.

Popular means well liked, prevalent, accepted, fashionable, common, and trendy. There is nothing wrong with being popular, as long as we do not allow popularity to control us. Popularity can have its own unique ups and downs, as any of us who went to high school know.

Popularity is built and lost much quicker than influence. We can incite people and build popularity. We can tell people what they want to hear and become popular. We can tell people things they shouldn't hear and become popular.

Influential, on the other hand, means powerful, important, persuasive, effective, forceful, and leading. For all practical purposes, we could be influential and yet relatively unknown in our culture's popular circles. I am convinced that in heaven we will discover that many who are the most influential in the courts of heaven were relatively unknown on the streets of earth. They are those who were willing to sow in secret, who spent more time on their faces talking to God than snapping selfies. To this end, I've set my heart on being influential.

Ideally, it would be wonderful to be both. I have a few friends who have managed to do this complicated dance brilliantly. But they never started out with the desire to be popular; they just wanted to be found faithful. This is exactly where all who desire to be witnesses of Christ should begin. Being faithful and influential means choosing our words with care and, as with the precious gift of grace, not using our freedom of speech as a license to sin.

Even though our government grants us the right to say whatever we want, ultimately we answer to a higher kingdom. Why should any of us be free with our opinions when we have been granted unrestrained access to the wisdom and insight of the Most High God? The Word of God is a diviner of thoughts and intent, not just thoughts without intent. Over the span of my life, I have frequently proven true the proverb that in a multitude of my words, something is bound to go amiss.

> When words are many, transgression is not lacking,
> but whoever restrains his lips is prudent.
> (Prov. 10:19)

I hope you agree that social media is not always healthy, and it is definitely not a family. On it we can see only what people choose to show us. Sometimes this means we see only their best and at other times only their worst. Sometimes everything they say and show us is a lie. I can't even begin to tell you how many people have pretended to be me and then asked for money for an orphanage that doesn't exist.

Virtual versus Actual

Honestly, it's far easier to invest in a virtual community than to cultivate an actual one. Typing sentences on a smartphone is far easier than having hard conversations with friends and family. Blogging allows us to sow words that produce immediate attention and positive feedback, while my actual community insists we practice patience because real conversations flow differently. One major difference is the need to allow others to speak.

Virtual communities can be good or bad, healthy or abusive. Healthy virtual communities encourage our engagement and relationships with our actual communities. If yours are doing this, they are a good thing.

There have never been so many winsome and persuasive bloggers. I follow a few blogs for specific areas such as healthy eating and leadership insights. Having said this, I am very careful who I allow to influence how I think. I want to know that they are accountable to someone or something. Popularity doesn't necessarily equate to accountability.

When we are lonely or struggling, we are easily pulled into the circles of others who are likewise lonely and struggling. Maybe we're dealing with postpartum depression or an eating disorder. We connect because there is common ground. It is good to know we're not alone and that someone understands us. These connections can be healthy and healing as long as they inevitably point us toward health and our truest source of strength. Where these communities go awry is when we allow others to think for us.

> **Popularity doesn't necessarily equate to accountability.**

Maybe we've connected with someone online in a way that started out healthy. We loved their cute personality, vulnerability, and incredible rawness. We liked how they said aloud what others only dared to think. We loved how their words were woven with such feeling. But if we do not anchor ourselves in community and in Scripture, it won't be long before how they feel about a matter becomes how we feel. It is okay for their questions to become ours as long as we know where to go for the answers.

For example, if a woman complains about not enjoying sex with her husband, do we simply question our enjoyment as well, or do we look for ways to build intimacy?

Maybe a blogger's marriage is over. The demise is written in poetic terms, and there is already the promise of a new start, a new mate. Rather than seeing divorce as the tearing of two souls, the blogger spins it into a victory for truth and love. When we are more emotionally involved with a virtual person than our own husbands, we run the risk of viewing our marriages in the light of their experience. We wonder if leaving our husbands might be the truly honest and bravest thing to do.

Okay, hit the pause button. Really?

Marriage is a covenant before God. If you don't like your marriage, cultivate it. Put down your phone, close your laptop, and leave behind the lies of comparison. Spend time with each other.

I am never going to advocate that you stay in a marriage in which you or your children are at risk or your spouse is unfaithful. I am speaking to situations in which you just aren't "feeling it" anymore. In this case, leaving may at first appear easier than doing the hard work to grow your relationship. But when God is in the process of remaking us into adamant, immovable, and invincible people who love well, easy isn't the route he chooses. He wants to build us up in word and strength.

Don't Go Public

Disagreements within the body of Christ are not a new thing. In his first letter to the church at Corinth, Paul wrote:

> And how dare you take each other to court! When you think you have been wronged, does it make any sense to go before a court that knows nothing of God's ways instead of a family of Christians? The day is coming when the world is going to stand before a jury made up of followers of Jesus. If someday you are going to rule on the world's fate, wouldn't it be a good idea to practice on some of these smaller cases? (6:1–2 Message)

Today taking someone to court could be likened to taking a private matter public. The pattern set in Scripture is that we go to those who've wronged us, first one-on-one and then with a friend. The posture we adopt is one of meekness, and the goal of the conversation is restoration and truth. Using social media as a justice system is an unbiblical nightmare. A mob has no regard for innocence or even accuracy.

Paul's letter to Timothy rings true as an urgent message for our time.

> Don't be naive. There are difficult times ahead. As the end approaches, people are going to be self-absorbed, money-hungry, self-promoting, stuck-up, profane, contemptuous of parents, crude, coarse, dog-eat-dog, unbending, slanderers, impulsively wild, savage, cynical, treacherous, ruthless, bloated windbags, addicted to lust, and allergic to God. They'll make a show of religion, but behind the scenes they're animals. Stay clear of these people. (2 Tim. 3:1–5 Message)

Sound familiar? Self-absorbed and money-hungry. Check. Self-promoting and stuck-up. Check. Profane, contemptuous of parents, crude, and coarse. Check. I fear there is not one for me to leave out. Paul goes on to warn Timothy what is at risk when this type of culture is the norm:

> These are the kind of people who smooth-talk themselves into the homes of unstable and needy women and take advantage of them; women who, depressed by their sinfulness, take up with every new religious fad that calls itself "truth." (2 Tim. 3:6 Message)

This passage is a hard one to hear . . . especially as a woman. To heed Paul's warning, we all need to take a deep breath and allow the Holy Spirit to frame this one for us. I think it is fair to say that this verse describes women living outside of healthy community and their God-given purpose. When any of us (male or female) are isolated and feel useless, we become easy prey to those who would take advantage of us. We all know we were made for more than the mundane. Boredom and depression can lead us to live vicariously through others. We comment on blogs, spend hours on social media, and get caught up in drama that is not our own. Let's be honest: it is easier to post opinions than it is to pray. When we know we're called to build something but lack opportunity, we are vulnerable to opportunists.

On the other hand, sometimes we become unstable and needy when we are overcommitted and have not created time to tend our souls. I can't tell you how many stories I have heard of both men and women who live extraordinarily busy lives that leave them utterly exhausted—who then begin affairs online.

My first reaction was, Who has time for that? You barely have time to talk with your spouse; how is it that you are writing essays to strangers? Then I realized that an online affair is an escape. It is a pretend place where they don't have to be responsible. Rather than edit their lives to make room, they self-sabotage.

It's time for some difficult family conversations. Shut the laptop. Put down the phone. Talk to your children. Engage with your spouse. Meet a friend for coffee. Speak to them on the phone. Make sure you are taking the time to invest in what is real.

Yes, the church needs to listen to the needs of its daughters. Women are hurting. The yearly women's gathering is good, but it is far from enough. Women tell me they are tired of studying and never doing, but taking our frustrations online is also not doing. Denouncing the things that aren't working isn't enough. Let's be part of building a healthy infrastructure for the body of Christ. Let's follow the example of Jesus's first followers, who ate and studied together. Going into all the world and making disciples begins with our immediate world.

In many churches, women have permission but not position. To change this, we need to sit down and have the right conversations with the right people. Online associations are great, but a writer, vlogger, or Facebook "friend" can't look you in the eye. Someone on Twitter can't hold you in their arms. We need people up close and personal. With so many words, we are depersonalizing far too many people who need Jesus.

> Going into all the world and making disciples begins with our immediate world.

As I worked on this chapter, Proverbs and Ecclesiastes served as a guide for becoming adamant in word. In appendix 2, I've included fifty proverbs to help you choose your words and what enters your mind so you can frame your life wisely.

Dear heavenly Father,
May I open my mouth with wisdom, and may the teaching of kindness be on my tongue (adapted from Prov. 31:26). Show me my family, who I can have heaven-breathed conversations about the concerns I carry. Forgive me for forgetting that you are committed to washing and readying your Bride. I will use my words to build rather than destroy, to heal rather than wound, to prophesy rather than criticize. Amen.

ADAMANT
TRANSFORMATION

Worship is the submission of all our nature to
God. It is the quickening of conscience by his holiness, the nourishment of the mind with his truth,
the purifying of the imagination by his beauty, the
opening of the heart to his love, the surrender of
the will to his purpose.

William Temple

Recently, I took three of my grandchildren cherry
picking in our neighborhood. I don't know if it was
because I have vision in only one eye or because I'd
forgotten what it's like to keep track of three little ones, but
it wasn't long before one of them was in danger. As I pulled
down a branch to put cherries within Sophia's grasp, she
yelled, "Lizzy!" and pointed in the direction of the street. I

turned in time to see Lizzy, who was two, waddle into the street. I let go of the branch and ran toward her. A car was headed her way.

I yelled, "Stop! Lizzy, come back!" Lizzy turned, eyes sparkling with mischief. She gave a winsome laugh and picked up her pace. She thought it was a game of chase. Arms flailing, I threw myself in the way of the oncoming car, doubting the driver could see Lizzy's chubby little form, and signaled the driver to stop since it was apparent that Lizzy had no intention of slowing.

I caught up with her in the median as she prepared to cross the second lane. I snatched her up in my arms and held her squirming form close to my racing heart. We waited in the safety of the median while the two-way traffic passed us before we crossed the street to join her brother and sister.

Lizzy continued to laugh, certain it had all been a grand adventure. After all, how could a two-year-old possibly know what a collision with a car would look like? Sophia, her five-year-old sister, had never experienced an encounter with a car, but she had a good idea that it was wrong—and I knew for certain it was dangerous and potentially deadly. You can be sure that for the remainder of the day Lizzy was in my arms or held firmly by the hand.

I'm quite certain that none of you would question my approach to Lizzy . . . safely in my arms or firmly by the hand. We all know the damage cars can do. My knowledge compelled me to rush into oncoming traffic and save Lizzy from herself.

In this chapter, I am going to leave the safety of the sidewalk and rush again into the perils of two-way traffic. I hope you will hear my heart, because if we don't allow our Lord to transform the way we think, live, and love, many people will never see his love or light in our lifetimes. We don't want to run the risk of living like Pharisees and laying burdens on a generation that we did nothing to lift (Matt. 23:4). We live in days that require wisdom and compassion. We are here to declare freedom to all who have been taken captive. We are agents of release. We are not prison guards, wardens, or judges who pick and choose who will be released. Conversely, the answer to the confusion of our day is not found in calling the prison a place of freedom.

> **We are here to declare freedom to all who have been taken captive.**

Planking

> Judge not, that you be not judged. For with the judgment you pronounce you will be judged, and with the measure you use it will be measured to you. Why do you see the speck that is in your brother's eye, but do not notice the log that is in your own eye? Or how can you say to your brother, "Let me take the speck out of your eye," when there is the log in your own eye? You hypocrite, first take the log out of your own eye, and then you will see clearly to take the speck out of your brother's eye. (Matt. 7:1–5)

As a former tax collector, Matthew knew exactly what it felt like to be judged by others. A takeaway from this passage is *don't judge!* This is good, but it is an incomplete rendering of this passage. Let's look a little closer at what is being said. When I first became a Christian, I felt so much judgment from other Christians that I tried to deflect it by counterjudging. For example, my double-pierced ears were considered scandalous and a form of self-mutilation. I countered by calling these Christians religious bigots. Thank God I didn't have access to a blog! My labels stayed within my head. And whose judgment was harsher? I am going to fall on the sword and say mine was.

My double-pierced ears confused them, but I condemned my accusers.

They had a speck, while I had enough wood in my eye to build an entertainment center. My log obstructed me from seeing their speck. To change this, a few things needed to happen. First step: I needed to admit I had a log.

A plank in the eye acts like a blindfold . . . all we see is the dark in others. Let's take this a bit further; no one wants someone who is blinded to perform any type of medical procedure on them. Let's remove our blindfolds and deal with our own issues so we can help rather than continue to hurt others.

You see, our judging friend in Matthew 7 was right: his brother did have a speck that needed removing. It is just that Jesus called him a hypocrite for deflecting and pointing out what was wrong when he was blind to his own state. Helping others in this state is counterproductive. The church points its finger at the world, while God wants us to allow his Word to hit us full force in the chest.

Has bemoaning the evils of our day gotten us anywhere?

The Bible is clear that a shift happens when we change our posture.

If my people who are called by my name humble themselves, and pray and seek my face and turn from their wicked ways, then I will hear from heaven and will forgive their sin and heal their land. (2 Chron. 7:14)

God looks at the posture of his people. This passage outlines an attitude of worship and repentance. Without love, we can be utterly right while horribly wrong.

Our land needs healing.

This healing begins with us.

It starts when God's people humble themselves, pray, seek God's face, and turn away from their own wicked ways. Do you realize how powerful this is? It doesn't matter who is in power. It doesn't matter what legislation is passed. We don't have to turn everyone else from their evil deeds . . . simply remove our own planks and then act accordingly.

Transformation begins as we own our issues and choose to live the truth. Transformation is not measured by the truth we know but is reflected in the truth we live. Love is key in our process of transformation. Without the factors of faith, hope, and love, transformation is impossible. This lack of love is the very reason there has been a move away from holiness and transformation.

> Transformation begins as we own our issues and choose to live the truth.

It is also why it is not popular now to say that anything or anyone could possibly be wrong. Even the church has adopted the more politically correct stance of saying that there are no absolutes and what is wrong for me might be right for you. This is not enough. A generation without convictions is a generation without transformation.

I want to change. This world needs me to change. Each and every day is another chance to follow Jesus and be changed into his likeness. I'm so grateful that God stripped me of the shame that covered me in order to robe me in his righteousness. Jesus didn't endorse my bondage by calling my shameful acts righteous. Nor did he call my filthy garments clean—he washed them in his Word.

Shame is never something that we are, but there are times when shame is something that we feel. There are times when our actions can only be called shameful. I have behaved in ways that were shameful. This doesn't make me shameful. This means I've said and done things that I'm ashamed of. When we allow shame to cause us to turn away from God, we attempt to cover ourselves with fig leaves and in turn blame those around us. We can choose to allow shame to separate us from God or to turn from the darkness and allow his light and love to bond us in a deeper manner to our Creator.

In the light of his love and holiness, God ultimately removes our shame.

My shame was not removed by me making excuses for my poor behavior and sin. I cannot look back and call my shameful practices honorable in light of my circumstances. My shame was removed when I turned away from a life of lies and chose to live in truth.

Transformation does not lie and deny our nakedness.

It does not call the naked clothed.

It does not hide from the presence of God behind fig leaves and trees.

Transformation begins as we admit our nakedness.

It confesses our failed attempts to try to cover ourselves in temporal trappings and the fig leaves of earth.

It admits that these never actually covered us.

It lays aside all vain human attempts and asks our holy Father to clothe us in truth.

When we come under Christ's lordship, we put away our shameful, self-willed practices and walk as children of light. Ephesians 4:21–25 describes this exchange:

> Since you have heard about Jesus and have learned the truth that comes from him, throw off your old sinful nature and your former way of life, which is corrupted by lust and deception. Instead, let the Spirit renew your thoughts and attitudes. Put on your new nature, created to be like God—truly righteous and holy. (NLT)

Throw it off! The Holy Spirit of grace empowers us to remove our former fallen nature and filthy shrouds of self-righteousness as though they were death shrouds. (Because they are!) Why would anyone want to put a new garment over a filthy old one? Sooner or later, the stain and the stink of the soiled garment would seep through and mar the new one. And none of us can bear the weight of wearing both. We cast off the old nature with its old patterns as we renew our minds and attitudes toward the godly and the holy.

Once we *know* better, we *do* better.

Once we *know* the truth (Jesus), we are empowered to *do* the truth.

Lust no longer has the right to distort our longings. Greed and deceitfulness of riches no longer have the right to veil our minds. Rather than call the old new, we renew.

Another Look at Tolerance

By itself, tolerance sounds humane. But what we tolerate in ourselves will not change; what we choose to be intentionally intolerant of will.

Recently, I was over at my son's house, and one of my grandchildren (who will remain unnamed) imagined it was a good idea to expand the uses of *hand* sanitizer. She fed it to a sibling who did not enjoy it and promptly told his father so. When her daddy heard about it, he was anything but tolerant of this practice. There was an immediate loving but firm conversation about the use of hand sanitizer. Her supply was confiscated until there was an assurance that hands would not be confused with mouths in the future.

> What we tolerate in ourselves will not change; what we choose to be intentionally intolerant of will.

Was her father being mean? Of course not! What *protects* the outside of our hands could very well *poison* the inside of our bodies. He was trying to keep those in his house safe. She didn't know better, but he did. When we know better, we instruct others. We can't expect a child to understand that not all liquids that smell good should be consumed. We have to teach them first so that they will know better in the future.

Please be brave in this moment and don't think of this truth in terms of others. Wrap it around yourself.

What do you tolerate or settle for in your own life?

What are some areas you need to be less tolerant of or even intolerant of in the future?

What is blocking you from transformation?

Imitate God

Ephesians 5 admonishes us:

> Imitate God, therefore, in everything you do, because you
> are his dear children. Live a life filled with love, following
> the example of Christ. He loved us and offered himself as
> a sacrifice for us, a pleasing aroma to God. (vv. 1–2 NLT)

I love how the Passion Translation expresses these verses
as well:

> Follow God and imitate all he does in everything you do,
> for then you will represent your Father as his beloved sons
> and daughters. And continue to walk surrendered to the
> extravagant love of Christ, for he surrendered his life as a
> sacrifice for us. His great love for us was pleasing to God,
> like an aroma of adoration—a sweet healing fragrance in
> heaven and earth.

These first two verses contain little to argue with. Paul has
just finished talking about the importance of kindness. We
all want to imitate our heavenly Father by behaving like his
Son, Jesus. This means first and foremost walking in love.
Jesus was the purest expression of love, but imitating Jesus
also means walking in purity, surrender, and obedience. The
very next verse goes on to describe what our conduct should
look like in a day saturated with the illicit and the impure:

> Let there be no sexual immorality, impurity, or greed among
> you. Such sins have no place among God's people. Obscene
> stories, foolish talk, and coarse jokes—these are not for you.
> Instead, let there be thankfulness to God. (Eph. 5:3–4 NLT)

The Passion Translation captures Ephesians 5:3–4 this way:

> This love has nothing to do with sexual immorality, lust, or greed—for you are his holy ones and let no one be able to accuse you of them in any form. Guard your speech. Forsake obscenities and worthless insults; these are nonsensical words that bring disgrace and are unnecessary. Instead, let worship fill your heart and spill out in your words as you remind each other of God's goodness.

I think we all know that people in the church can be very mean-spirited at times. Rather than embracing these Scripture passages to purify ourselves, we use them to persecute those we've deemed more guilty. The limits of love and accountability have been blurred. For the most part, this is because people (Christians) have not loved or lived the truth well. I know you want to see this change.

To help us love and live the truth well, I want to unpack three ideas from the book of Romans:

1. the reality of our God
2. the reality of our day
3. the reality of us

The third point is where I intend to spend the greater portion of our study. It is there that we will examine our hearts and remove the planks.

I am going to cite each Scripture passage from two versions—the English Standard Version and the Message—in order that what might be unclear in one might be made clear in the other. First let's tackle the reality of our God.

The Reality of Our God

For what can be known about God is plain to them, because God has shown it to them. For his invisible attributes, namely, his eternal power and divine nature, have been clearly perceived, ever since the creation of the world, in the things that have been made. So they are without excuse. (Rom. 1:19–20)

But the basic reality of God is plain enough. Open your eyes and there it is! By taking a long and thoughtful look at what God has created, people have always been able to see what their eyes as such can't see: eternal power, for instance, and the mystery of his divine being. So nobody has a good excuse. (Message)

Everything we see declares the existence of the unseen God. All that we know reveals the reality of the unknown. Creation reveals a God of wonder and boundless creativity. If no one ever told us there was a Creator, the symphony of nature would draw our eyes and ears to his existence. All that is made reveals the One without maker. Our God alone is supreme. He is the Lord thy God, the alone and the above all. The Psalms paint such magnificent descriptions of the God Most High:

All that is made reveals the One without maker.

For God is great, and worth a thousand Hallelujahs. His terrible beauty makes the gods look cheap; pagan gods are mere tatters and rags. God made the heavens—royal splendor radiates from him, a powerful beauty sets him apart. (Ps. 96:4–6 Message)

And:

> Fire blazes out before him, flaming high up the craggy mountains. His lightnings light up the world; earth, wide-eyed, trembles in fear. The mountains take one look at GOD and melt, melt like wax before earth's Lord. (Ps. 97:3–5 Message)

It is impossible to read these verses and somehow miss the awe.

The Reality of Our Day

When I pause and consider the reality of our day, I find myself asking the recurring question, "Father, what has happened?" As we continue reading in the book of Romans, the following verses address how a shift has occurred:

> For although they knew God, they did not honor him as God or give thanks to him, but they became futile in their thinking, and their foolish hearts were darkened. Claiming to be wise, they became fools. (1:21–22)

And from the Message:

> What happened was this: People knew God perfectly well, but when they didn't treat him like God, refusing to worship him, they trivialized themselves into silliness and confusion so that there was neither sense nor direction left in their lives. They pretended to know it all, but were illiterate regarding life.

When we dishonor God and undermine who he is with the expression of our lives, we inevitably trivialize ourselves into an illiterate life. This means we read but never truly understand. With all of creation declaring his reality, it is hard not to acknowledge that there is a Creator, but knowing *about* God is a very different thing than *worshiping* him. It is one thing to acknowledge his existence and quite another to bow the knee. We can only know God in the worship of him. When we dishonor what we were created to honor, our thinking gets off-kilter. The word choice of the English Standard Version is *futile*; it means to be useless, vain, and barren. This describes thinking without utility or the ability to build. The Message paraphrase of this verse reads, "They pretended to know it all, but were illiterate regarding life."

The reality of our day weighs on us all. There has never been a generation with more access to information and yet with less clarity of purpose. We have some very real challenges when it comes to healthy relational connections. We develop virtual personas at the expense of our actual relational connections. We have learned to flit from one thing to another, rarely staying long enough in one place before we are pulled away. The concept of pondering and pausing to worship has become a lost art.

The concept of pondering and pausing to worship has become a lost art.

The book of Romans goes on to say what happens when we refuse to worship God and spend ourselves on other things:

> [They] exchanged the glory of the immortal God for images resembling mortal man and birds and animals and creeping things. Therefore God gave them up in the lusts of their

hearts to impurity, to the dishonoring of their bodies among themselves, because they exchanged the truth about God for a lie and worshiped and served the creature rather than the Creator, who is blessed forever! Amen. (1:23–25)

And from the Message:

They traded the glory of God who holds the whole world in his hands for cheap figurines you can buy at any roadside stand. So God said, in effect, "If that's what you want, that's what you get." It wasn't long before they were living in a pigpen, smeared with filth, filthy inside and out. And all this because they traded the true God for a fake god, and worshiped the god they made instead of the God who made them—the God we bless, the God who blesses us. Oh, yes!

Our Western culture has exchanged the glory of the eternal realm for the immediate gratification of what we can buy, touch, and control. We have largely spurned the Creator, who would lift us higher, and turned to the worship of his creation, which draws us lower. Turning our hearts to the idols of ambition and greed, we have debased ourselves with sexual impurity.

Before you jump to the conclusion that this describes a limited sector, consider what author Preston Sprinkle shares in his book *People to Be Loved*: "The reference to 'sexual impurity' here is not limited to same-sex relations. It's a general statement that includes sex outside of marriage, adultery, rape, and all sorts of other sexual sins committed by both gay and straight people."[1]

My guilt is found in this list. I came from a long line of fornicators. Honestly, pornography and perversion in every form have become popular. The Western world has awakened in a pigpen and wondered how they arrived in such a state.

When we turn from God, his restraining hand is removed and we are released to go our own way. This truth is not unlike what happened to the children of Israel as they sojourned through the wilderness. They lost the wonder of God's provision of manna and demanded meat. They thought the meat would strengthen their frames. God gave them quail, but with it came a fragility of soul. When we demand our own way, we often lose ourselves. As Paul writes:

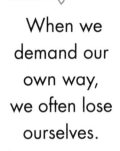

When we demand our own way, we often lose ourselves.

> For this reason God gave them up to dishonorable passions. For their women exchanged natural relations for those that are contrary to nature; and the men likewise gave up natural relations with women and were consumed with passion for one another, men committing shameless acts with men and receiving in themselves the due penalty for their error. (Rom. 1:26–27)

And:

> Worse followed. Refusing to know God, they soon didn't know how to be human either—women didn't know how to be women, men didn't know how to be men. Sexually confused, they abused and defiled one another, women with women, men with men—all lust, no love. And then they paid for it, oh, how they paid for it—emptied of God and love, godless and loveless wretches. (Message)

There is an awful lot in these two verses, but each sentence points to the fact that none of us know how to be human outside the wisdom of our Creator. It is in the knowledge of God that we find our humanity. It is the knowledge of God that keeps us free from defiling ourselves no matter what form that debasement might take (adultery, greed, cruelty, fornication, etc.).

Yet I fear our culture has forgotten the basics. Most American movies celebrate violence—and then we are surprised when we see violence in our homes, schools, and streets. TV programming, not to mention commercials, promotes sex of all kinds. We are exposed to far more than we should be, and this exposure has triggered things the previous generations never had to deal with on a daily basis.

Our public education systems are being pressured to encourage middle school–age children to self-identify their gender at possibly the most confusing time period in their lives. Have we all forgotten how rough junior high was? (It's been a long time, but I still remember how traumatic it was!)

If someone would have asked me to self-identify in junior high, I would have said I was a unicorn. I was just trying to figure out what was going on with my own body and the reason why I wasn't growing breasts. I would have rather looked at girls in the locker room to sort through this confusing season than peek at the boys.

It is normal to have same-sex curiosity during this time period; everyone is trying to figure out what is happening to their bodies. Why aren't we protecting this process? Why are we sexualizing our youth?

You don't ask people who are transitioning from boy to man or girl to woman to self-identify. Are we really going to allow the school systems and our culture to sexualize our children and pervert their puberty? Some schools are even showing same-sex interactions of girls kissing girls and boys kissing boys and telling children that if they have a sexual response to what they see, it is because they are gay.

No. If they have a sexual response, it is because God wired us to respond sexually to sexual interactions, period. When we see something sexual, our bodies have a sexual reaction. This is true whether we are married or single, straight or gay, old or young. It doesn't mean we will cheat on our mates or even that we want to have sex with the people we saw having sex.

Within the covenant of marriage, the passion between a man and a woman is honorable. Outside of marriage, the honorable becomes dishonorable. This is the reason why adultery and fornication are considered a breach of covenant. Then there are the passions the Bible refers to in the various translations as unnatural and dishonorable. These include homosexuality, incest, pedophilia, and bestiality. And here is where I must pause. Romans 1 reminds us—all have sinned. Greed and slander are just as grievous as adultery and homosexuality.

The Cost of Sin

Romans 1:27 continues with the mention of a penalty or cost to those who yield to this mind-set. I want to be clear that it is *never* God who makes us pay. He is the one who invites us to transformation—to choose life and blessing rather than death and curses. He invites all of us prodigals who wake up in the pigpen of a squandered life to return to the Father, where a robe, ring, and feast await our homecoming. He is our *even-now* God who says, "Come now, let us reason together . . . though your sins are like scarlet, they shall be as white as snow" (Isa. 1:18). It doesn't matter what we have done or with whom we have done it. He will redeem us.

It doesn't matter what we have done or with whom we have done it. He will redeem us.

But when we build our lives with the untempered mortar of idolatry, sexual sin, and greed, our lives will eventually collapse, and the wreck is costly. When we spend everything in the hope that another person, another gender, another drug, another car, another house, or another addiction will finally satisfy us, we set ourselves up for failure. The broken people of our day are so desperate for wholeness that they are willing to go to the furthest extremes, and part of the reason is because we are not modeling our transformation well.

Romans continues:

And since they did not see fit to acknowledge God, God gave them up to a debased mind to do what ought not to be done. (1:28)

And from the Message:

Since they didn't bother to acknowledge God, God quit bothering them and let them run loose.

We are a people running loose. We ran from the restraints of a loving Father only to discover ourselves shackled to ruin. We are like the children of Israel when everyone did what was right in their own eyes. The next few verses in Romans describe in detail what a people without any God restraint might look like:

> We ran from the restraints of a loving Father only to discover ourselves shackled to ruin.

They [all who refuse to worship God] were filled with all manner of unrighteousness, evil, covetousness, malice. They are full of envy, murder, strife, deceit, maliciousness. They are gossips, slanderers, haters of God, insolent, haughty, boastful, inventors of evil, disobedient to parents, foolish, faithless, heartless, ruthless. (1:29–31)

And from the Message:

And then all hell broke loose: rampant evil, grabbing and grasping, vicious backstabbing. They made life hell on earth with their envy, wanton killing, bickering, and cheating. Look at them: mean-spirited, venomous, fork-tongued God-bashers. Bullies, swaggerers, insufferable windbags! They keep inventing new ways of wrecking lives. They ditch their parents when they get in the way. Stupid, slimy, cruel, cold-blooded.

And after this heartbreaking list of what a culture that refuses to honor and worship God looks like, Paul concludes his description with verse 32:

Though they know God's righteous decree that those who practice such things deserve to die, they not only do them but give approval to those who practice them.

And it's not as if they don't know better. They know perfectly well they're spitting in God's face. And they don't care—worse, they hand out prizes to those who do the worst things best! (Message)

The truth is we all deserved death. But until recently, we never dreamed of asking others to approve of or even reward the destructive patterns of our former lifestyle choices (greed, immorality, pride, gossip, jealousy, etc.). When we accepted Christ, grace empowered us to leave behind these practices that positioned us under the wrath of God. We cannot misuse Scripture passages on grace to validate what compromised us in the past. This ends the reality of our day. Now for the adamantly important part.

The Reality of Us

But we are ultimately not children of our day—we are children of eternity. So let's move from what is into what could be as we tackle the reality of us, which opens up before us in Romans 2:

Therefore you have no excuse, O man, every one of you who judges. For in passing judgment on another you condemn yourself, because you, the judge, practice the very same things. We know that the judgment of God rightly falls on those who practice such things. Do you suppose, O man—you who judge those who practice such things and yet do them yourself—that you will escape the judgment of God? (vv. 1–3)

And from the Message:

Those people are on a dark spiral downward. But if you think that leaves you on the high ground where you can point your finger at others, think again. Every time you criticize someone, you condemn yourself. It takes one to know one. Judgmental criticism of others is a well-known way of escaping detection in your own crimes and misdemeanors. But God isn't so easily diverted. He sees right through all such smoke screens and holds you to what you've done. You didn't think, did you, that just by pointing your finger at others you would distract God from seeing all your misdoings and from coming down on you hard?

No Excuses

There it is again. We are never positioned to judge. Never. For far too long, we have tried to distract God from our own failings rather than lifting Jesus through our transformed lives. God alone is the Judge of one and all. Perhaps our sins are of a different nature, but this doesn't mean God will not hold us to what we have done. Perhaps we are not involved in sexual sin . . . but what about the rest of the list? What about

We are never positioned to judge. Never.

offenses such as slander, envy, strife, gossip, bragging, and greed? Are these not rampant in the church?

We all need mercy, so let's extend mercy.

We all need love, so let's extend love.

We all need hope and people who see the potential of who we might be. Loving people and extending mercy set all of us up for transformation.

Paul goes on to explain how transformation happens.

Or do you presume on the riches of his kindness and for-bearance and patience, not knowing that God's kindness is meant to lead you to repentance? (2:4)

And:

Or did you think that because he's such a nice God, he'd let you off the hook? Better think this one through from the beginning. God is kind, but he's not soft. In kindness he takes us firmly by the hand and leads us into a radical life-change. (Message)

> God's kindness is always an invitation for us to return to truth, rather than an endorsement of sin.

God's kindness is always an invitation for us to return to truth, rather than an endorsement of sin. C. S. Lewis writes, "The hardness of God is kinder than the softness of man, and his compulsion is our liberation."[2] God ultimately desires to lead us firmly into freedom by the pathway of truth. Jesus was raised from the dead so that we could walk away from our ignorance and live in a way that honors his sacrifice (Acts 17:30–31).

Let's talk about this idea of being taken firmly by the hand and led into a life of radical change. I don't know what this means for you, so I'll begin by telling you about the day God took me firmly by the hand.

Born Again

I was born again at the age of twenty-one when I was home attending summer school at Purdue. Up until then, my life was on the very dark downward spiral described in Romans. I was mean, willful, promiscuous, and rebellious. Then one night during a picnic that turned into a Bible study, the scales came off my eyes. Surrounded by people who were lifting their hands while they sang off-key, I didn't know where to look. To escape their sincere faces and uplifted hands, I looked down at the song sheet. I read ahead to the words of the next song, "Robes of Righteousness." In one of the verses, I read that it was possible for God to look at me but no longer see me; he'd see Jesus.

In that moment, I heard the Holy Spirit whisper, "I can't look at you." As I read the words, I realized Jesus was the covering I needed. Up until that time, I had reasoned away my actions and choices with a myriad of excuses and blame.

That night I prayed to be born again, and I surrendered my life to the leading of God's Holy Spirit. When I returned to my dorm room, I had such a sense that there were things in my room that were incongruent with my new life. I lost no time in dumping these items in the garbage down the hall.

No one had told me to do this. When God's Spirit filled me, I began to feel things I had never felt before. Actions, words, and behavior patterns that I had embraced as normal now felt awkward and at times grievous. This was not the sway of shame or even guilt over my life. It was the presence of a new influence and a sense of the consciousness of a Holy God.

John (my future husband) had continually quoted Paul the apostle to me. I remembered that the college had placed a copy of *The Way*, an edition of the New Testament, in my room. I spent quite a bit of time looking for the book of Paul that night. I stood the Bible on its spine and prayed for it to open to the book of Paul. The pages parted to reveal these words in 2 Corinthians 5:17:

> Therefore, if anyone is in Christ, he is a new creation. The old has passed away; behold, the new has come.

When I realized that these were the words of Paul, I thought I had found the only chapter he had authored! I fell asleep in peace for the first time in a decade.

Something Happened

I awoke early the next morning aware that my spirit was alive. I scrambled off my top bunk to go tell my mother what had happened. Immediately, I heard these chilling words: "Nothing happened last night. You're no different." I froze in terror. I began to question it myself. Who was I kidding . . . me a Christian? Then I remembered the peace I'd experienced and how I'd slept for the first time in a long time without the use of alcohol, how after prayer I'd literally felt the knots in my stomach untie as the healing warmth of God's love entered my body.

It was then that I recognized his voice.

This was the voice of the destroyer.

It was the same voice that had driven me to an eating disorder. It was the voice that had overwhelmed me with fear and insecurity. It was the voice that had isolated and accused me. It was the voice that had lured me to sin.

Had this voice ever told me I wasn't a Christian? Never. Not one time had it raised the question of my eternal standing. In that moment, I realized that liars and thieves do not come to steal what we do not have. This was the first morning I was saved, which is why there were whispers of doubt.

But the words had the very opposite effect on me. Rather than undermining what had happened the night before, they served only to confirm the truth.

Something had happened! I almost laughed out loud. The presence of the enemy served to reveal the reality of my God.

I was going to have to go so far out on a limb that there was no coming back. I couldn't hint about a change in my life. I committed right then and there to be all in with God. I was water baptized within the next two weeks.

A month later when I went back to my sorority house in Arizona for the fall term, I let my sisters know what had happened in my life over the summer. Needless to say, not everyone was happy about it and not everyone was convinced.

Knocks on My Door

I was reading my Bible aloud in my room one day when I heard loud footsteps in the hallway followed by a knock on my door. I opened the door to a sorority sister who told me to "Stop reading aloud!" She seemed just as startled by her words as I was. I knew then that demons were real. To respect my sorority sisters, I climbed the fire escape and read my Bible aloud on the roof of our house.

From this vantage, I declared the promises of God over the campus, the house, and my future. Many nights I felt led to walk the halls and quietly pray for my sisters, calling them out of the domain of darkness and into the kingdom of light.

It wasn't long before there were other knocks on my door. Freshman girls wanted to know what had happened to me. They had heard how I used to be and had seen how I now was, and they wanted what I had. I grabbed a tract I had from Campus Crusade and had them repeat the entire tract aloud word for word.

I remember the first time I preached to my sorority sisters. It came at an unexpected time. For some reason, I thought international economics was a good major choice. The first few years were easy enough, but in my junior and senior years, the professors were beginning to weed out the weak.

A few of us who were in the same courses had pulled an all-nighter studying for midterms. Now we were at the breakfast table cramming and quizzing one another. I was ramped up on NoDoz and coffee when in waltzed one of my sorority sisters who had wisely chosen the major I should have pursued as the future mother of four boys: elementary education. She took one look at us and let us know that we looked awful. We paused to receive her input and returned to our studies. But she didn't get the hint. She got her tray of food and joined us. She said something to the effect of, "Lisa, you look like you've been run over by a car."

All I remember was a tremor, and the unregenerate Lisa began to rise to the surface. Then out of my mouth came the question I'd been thinking about for the last few years: "Why are you such a [bleep] in the morning?"

The breakfast room froze . . . the born-again had cussed. Before I was a Christian, I had cussed all the time, but as a new believer, I had managed to cuss only in my head. Now it was out there in the open, and most of my sisters didn't know what to do. But this sister did. She stood up, pointed her finger at me, announced, "I knew it! I knew there was no way you could have become a Christian. You're just too bad!" and stormed out of the now-silent room.

I started to stand up, and my sweet roommate grabbed my arm and assured me, "I was just about to say the same thing."

I smiled and rose to my feet; all eyes were now on me. My next words were, "I owe all of you an apology. I was completely out of line."

Later, many of my friends said that was the moment they actually knew I'd become a Christian. You see, they didn't hear me praying in the shower or reading my Bible out loud on the roof. They didn't see me walking the halls at night praying for them. That day, for the very first time, they saw me humble myself.

> We will all make mistakes, but we are not allowed to make excuses.

Isn't it possible that this is the posture—a position of humility—we all need to adopt if we are going to model adamant transformation? We will all make mistakes, but we are not allowed to make excuses. As we know to do better, we do better. And when we do worse, we own it.

Charles Spurgeon said:

> You cannot preach conviction of sin unless you have suffered it. You cannot preach repentance unless you have practiced it. You cannot preach faith unless you have exercised it. True preaching is artesian; it wells up from the great depths of the soul. If Christ has not made a well within us, there will be no outflow from us.[3]

I love this. True preaching is artesian—it is a spring of living water. Mercy should flow unhindered from each of us!

Dear heavenly Father,
Take me firmly by the hand and lead me into a radical
life change. I want every part of my life to be a message
that points others to you. I want to be known by what
you are for rather than by what I am against. I will no
longer make excuses for my messes. Convict me of the
areas that contradict your work in my life.

10

ADAMANT IN HOLINESS

Holiness is the perfection of all [God's] other
attributes. His power is holy power, his mercy
is holy mercy, his wisdom is holy wisdom. It is
his holiness more than any other attribute that
makes him worthy of our praise.

Jerry Bridges

I remember reading *The Pursuit of Holiness* when I was
in my early twenties. Each page spoke to an unrealized
longing within me. I understood that God was holy, but
the idea that I could pursue holiness had been lost on me.
With this realization, the wording of my journal changed, my
focus in worship shifted, I even chose my friends differently.
This was not because I imagined myself better than anyone
else. In truth, I knew I was weaker and far more susceptible
to the sway of all things unholy.

For this reason, I took great pains to guard what had been revealed to me so that the Holy One might be revealed through me. My bent had always been toward the wild side—only for me to discover that it was a way of life that was a slow death. In reaction, I went repressively tame for a bit too long and found myself tangled up in rules and the import of appearances. By the time I had given birth to my first child, I carried a deep desire for him to be at once holy and free—this meant his mother would need to experience the same thing herself.

The pursuit of holiness is our release.

Fear not! Embracing the concept of holiness does not add yet another list of rules to restrain us. Far from it . . . the pursuit of holiness is our release. It is the assurance that there is more to the Christian life than a confession of righteousness. Holiness is an invitation into the adamant wholeness of God. Scottish theologian Sinclair Ferguson writes:

> God's holiness means he is separate from sin. But holiness in God also means wholeness. God's holiness is his "God-ness." It is his being God in all that it means for him to be God. To meet God in his holiness, therefore, is to be altogether overwhelmed by the discovery that he is God, and not man.[1]

God is separate from sin, yet through Christ he is as close as our breath. When we pause in his holy presence, there is a revelation of how very unlike us he is and at the same time a deep awareness of how very much he loves us. In many ways, choosing to walk in holiness is our response to his gift of righteousness. He has robed us in radiance—why would we wear it to wallow again in the mud? We are loved by the King who gave his Son to lift our heads out of our darkness so that we might behold his light. Why would any of us want to revisit the realms of shadow?

God is holy and God does holy.

Just like his love, God's holiness is adamant: invincible, unassailable, indivisible, impenetrable, constant, unshakable, and insistent.

His holiness is unyielding and attractive—for God's holiness is as beautiful in terror as it is in tenderness.

God is holy light. God is holy love. God is a holy consuming fire.

Holiness cannot be separated from the transcendent nature of God.

God is our holy Father who reigns in holiness and awesome, holy wonder. From the Old Testament to the New, the holiness of God is proclaimed:

> Who is like you, O LORD, among the gods? Who is like you, majestic in holiness, awesome in glorious deeds, doing wonders? (Exod. 15:11)

And:

> Who will not fear, O Lord, and glorify your name? For you alone are holy. All nations will come and worship you, for your righteous acts have been revealed. (Rev. 15:4)

What Is Holiness?

To move forward with this adamant attribute of God, we first need to understand it. The word *holy* is defined in part as "perfect in goodness" and "righteousness." Most commonly, holiness refers to a transcendent otherness, behavior that is outside and far superior to the common behaviors of man. Because God is holy in all he is, he is holy in all he does. The behavior of the Holy One is holiness. Other words for holy are sanctified, consecrated, purified, dedicated, godly, and sacred.

> Because God is holy in all he is, he is holy in all he does.

In the words of N. T. Wright, "People have often regarded holiness as a negative quality—the absence of moral fault—but it is actually a positive thing, the shining reflection that appears in human character when we learn in practice what it means to be in God's image."[2]

I love this. Holiness is learned as we practically work out what it means to live as a child of the Most High God.

God is holy in grace, holy in power, holy in faith, holy in love, holy in truth, holy in knowledge, and holy in judgment. Our God always was holy, is now holy, and will always be holy. Yet he invites us who have not been holy, who possibly are not even now acting holy, to be holy. This is not an invitation for us to attempt and fail at human goodness. Because we are his own, we've been granted the divine privilege of being partakers of his holy nature.

Here is the promise given in 2 Peter 1:3–4:

> His divine power has granted to us all things that pertain to life and godliness, through the knowledge of him who called us to his own glory and excellence, by which he has granted to us his precious and very great promises, so that through them you may become partakers of the divine nature, having escaped from the corruption that is in the world because of sinful desire.

His divine power has graced us with *all* that we need to walk in godliness and holiness. Nothing went missing. We have his promise that we have been equipped with *everything* we need to practice holiness. Christ won us the promise as surely as he set the pattern. Charles Spurgeon wrote, "In holiness God is more clearly seen than in anything else, save in the Person of Christ Jesus the Lord, of whose life such holiness is but a repetition."[3]

Jesus expressed the holiness of the Father. When it comes to holiness, Jesus is both our pattern and our high priest. Because he and God are one, Jesus did and said only what he heard and saw his holy Father say and do. This is the pattern for our life of worship.

This is why Paul asks us:

What agreement has the temple of God with idols? For we are the temple of the living God; as God said, "I will make my dwelling among them and walk among them, and I will be their God, and they shall be my people. Therefore go out from their midst, and be separate from them, says the Lord, and touch no unclean thing; then I will welcome you, and I will be a father to you, and you shall be sons and daughters to me, says the Lord Almighty." (2 Cor. 6:16–18)

To answer Paul's first question: none. There is no accord. Using the Aramaic, the Passion Translation puts a finer point on this and asks, "What friendship does God's temple have with demons?" The answer should be easy enough . . . none! Paul admonishes us further:

Since we have these promises, beloved, let us cleanse ourselves from every defilement of body and spirit, bringing holiness to completion in the fear of God. (2 Cor. 7:1)

I recently read an insightful article that challenged the current thinking of the Wesleyan Church in light of the mind-set of its founder. Here is an excerpt:

> Christians in the Wesleyan/Methodist tradition ought to particularly refuse to choose between forgiveness (justification) and holiness (sanctification), as Wesley himself was adamant that both were part of the Christian life. In her recent book, *Discovering Christian Holiness: The Heart of Wesleyan-Holiness Theology*, Diane Leclerc suggests that over the last generation Wesleyans have not been very good stewards of the message of holiness. She points to a crisis, which is not a crisis over how to communicate holiness, but a more devastating crisis of silence, "the lack of articulation of holiness." As a result, Leclerc finds that "the pendulum seems to have swung from legalism to pessimism about victory over sin. Many of my students believe that sin is inevitable, pervasive, and enduring in a Christian's life. Sadly, they seem to be unaware of a different way to live.[4]

When I read this, hope came alive. Holiness involves both justification and sanctification, and the coupling of these brings wholeness.

Living Holy

Holiness in What We Do

Strive for peace with everyone, and for the holiness without which no one will see the Lord. See to it that no one fails to obtain the grace of God; that no "root of bitterness" springs up and causes trouble, and by it many become defiled; that no one is sexually immoral or unholy like Esau, who sold his birthright for a single meal. (Heb. 12:14–16)

Strife does not foster holiness. God's holy presence will not abide among the disjointed and the divisive. In his holiness, he cannot bless the offended and the unforgiving even though he longs to. Sexual immorality in all its forms will isolate us. And may the lesson that came at great cost to Esau teach each of us to treasure legacy more than the immediacy of appetite.

Because God is holy in all he is, he invites us to be holy in all we do.

Holiness in What We Think

Now this I say and testify in the Lord, that you must no longer walk as the Gentiles do, in the futility of their minds. They are darkened in their understanding, alienated from the life of God because of the ignorance that is in them, due to their hardness of heart. They have become callous and have given themselves up to sensuality, greedy to practice every kind of impurity. (Eph. 4:17–19)

As we learned, futility is the opposite of utility. Our minds reason according to what they have known and experienced; this can actually work against the purpose of transformation. We cannot return to the patterns we developed when we were strangers to the life of God. We were dying then as we indulged in idolatry and debauchery in the hope that they would make us feel alive. Those who are desensitized must dive deeper and deeper into the darkness of the sensual realm. Ephesians continues to point us to Jesus:

> But that is not the way you learned Christ!—assuming that you have heard about him and were taught in him, as the truth is in Jesus, to put off your old self, which belongs to your former manner of life and is corrupt through deceitful desires, and to be renewed in the spirit of your minds, and to put on the new self, created after the likeness of God in true righteousness and holiness. (4:20–24)

There it is again. We are admonished to throw aside our old self, its manner of life and all its accompanying cravings, that we would make way for a new true self. The new self is the one the Holy Spirit longs to reveal to us in true righteousness (right standing) and true holiness (how to live in light of this righteousness). N. T. Wright affirms this in his commentary on the prison letters of Paul:

> "Be renewed in the spirit of your mind" (v. 23): that's the secret. If the heart is right, it's time to get the mind right. Then you'll have the energy of will-power to bring the behaviour into line. Off with the old, on with the new![5]

And how do we renew the spirit of our minds? This is a question I am asked all the time, but my answer is not always what people want to hear. Our minds are renewed by obedience to the truth of God's Word. Let's dive into 1 Peter to surround this directive with context.

Holiness Is Obedience

Therefore, preparing your minds for action, and being sober-minded, set your hope fully on the grace that will be brought to you at the revelation of Jesus Christ. As obedient children, do not be conformed to the passions of your former ignorance, but as he who called you is holy, you also be holy in all your conduct, since it is written, "You shall be holy, for I am holy." (1 Pet. 1:13–16)

While studying this charge to prepare our minds for action, I found alongside it the phrase "girding up the loins of your mind." It is a call to renew and arm our minds with God's Word so that our hope is firmly anchored in the empowerment of grace. This grace brings both a revelation and a willingness to follow Jesus Christ.

Obedience will require that we choose what and whom we will obey. Will we obey our passions or the Word of God that framed our very lives? Our spirits are willing, but our flesh is weak and in the habit of sinning. Therefore, we must intentionally choose to make the shift toward obedience on every level. As we read the Word, we pray that the Holy Spirit will reveal any areas of conformity and compromise that we may be tolerating out of habit or ignorance.

Once we know, we do.

I share this to encourage you; I rarely *feel* like obeying. I obey because I choose to honor God. The admonishment here is that, as he who called us is holy, we also should be holy in all our conduct. God is holy in all he is. We are to be holy in all we do. This means the way we live before others should reflect our submission to our unseen God.

God is holy . . . we do holy.

> **God is holy . . .**
> **we do holy.**

Having purified your souls by your obedience to the truth for a sincere brotherly love, love one another earnestly from a pure heart, since you have been born again, not of perishable seed but of imperishable, through the living and abiding word of God. (1 Pet. 1:22–23)

Obedience to truth purifies our souls. This purification happens through doing, not merely hearing. We are saved through the sacrifice of the spotless Lamb and our minds are renewed by the Word and our souls are purified through obedience to truth. It is progressive.

As we obey truth, our hearts are refined so that we can love one another deeply. Love cannot go deeper than the room the heart makes for it. Abiding in God's Word increases our depth and capacity to truly love. A heart that resists truth can only love superficially. Christ is that imperishable seed and our adamant Cornerstone of all truth. Outside of truth, love is impossible.

> Abiding in God's Word increases our depth and capacity to truly love.

The incorruptible seed of God's Word endures forever. A pursuit of holiness is not even possible outside of God's Word. This pursuit is not subject to our interpretation. When the Word has its way in us, we love and produce fruit that remains because it is holy and true. There will be times when obedience to truth will feel like a death in this realm. But remember, friends, our days on earth are but a vapor. We will wake to discover our true lives in the next.

Holiness is our connection with an eternal perspective.

Holiness is our otherworldliness.

These verses return us to the Cornerstone and what it means to be part of the living Stone and a holy people.

Holiness Builds a Life That Honors God

So put away all malice and all deceit and hypocrisy and envy and all slander. Like newborn infants, long for the pure spiritual milk, that by it you may grow up into salvation—if indeed you have tasted that the Lord is good. (1 Pet. 2:1–3)

Salvation is a free gift (rather than earned) that we grow into each day. It is as though each of us were given a house that is empty. We are in the house (saved), but it is in need of furnishings so that we can live comfortably and invite others in. As we taste God's goodness, we grow in goodness. And then Peter says:

Welcome to the living Stone, the source of life. The workmen took one look and threw it out; God set it in the place of honor. (1 Pet. 2:4 Message)

Holiness Means We Control Our Bodies

For this is the will of God, your sanctification: that you abstain from sexual immorality; that each one of you know how to control his own body in holiness and honor, not in the passion of lust like the Gentiles who do not know God; that no one transgress and wrong his brother in this matter, because the Lord is an avenger in all these things, as we told you beforehand and solemnly warned you. For God has not called us for impurity, but in holiness. Therefore whoever disregards this, disregards not man but God, who gives his Holy Spirit to you. (1 Thess. 4:3–8)

It is the will of God that we are not only saved but also sanctified. When we know God, we allow his Word to govern our lives, and we no longer live by our past proclivity or by the dictates of our culture. The Thessalonians lived in a highly promiscuous culture; mistresses, ritual sex, catamites, and prostitutes were their cultural norm. To stay strong in this riot of sin, believers needed to be examples of godliness to one another. Paul did not make excuses for the Thessalonians because of their culture; he believed that the grace of God was powerful enough for them to walk in holiness.

We are being watched. How we live shows what we believe. If we live in such a way that causes others to stumble and sin, God will rise up on their behalf.

Second Timothy says:

> Now in a great house there are not only vessels of gold and silver but also of wood and clay, some for honorable use, some for dishonorable. Therefore, if anyone cleanses himself from what is dishonorable, he will be a vessel for honorable use, set apart as holy, useful to the master of the house, ready for every good work. So flee youthful passions and pursue righteousness, faith, love, and peace, along with those who call on the Lord from a pure heart. (2:20–22)

We're in the house. So why not make ourselves as useful and as valuable to the Master of the house as possible?

So many areas of my life required a long preparation process. For example, it was a long time before I could speak on marriage. In this and other areas, I was not yet ready; I was not yet useful for my Master's purposes. In these areas, I was a work in progress rather than fit for good works. The only trophy I ever got was when I was ten. It was for Most Improved. That pretty much is the story of my life. For the most part, we forget that improving is winning.

I have a heart to see a generation of youth made ready faster. This means they must *flee* their youthful passions. Flee means to run from as if in terror. Leave lust, pride, comparison, and competition in the dust. Running away isn't enough. We must run to something. It is time to run toward adamant righteousness, faith, love, and peace. I want young men and women counted among those who call on the Lord with a pure heart. I want the name of the Lord to be the strong tower for every generation, and his name is holy.

Holiness means we approach God on his terms, not our own. Our culture has adopted the practice of taking the grace of God and using it as a license to sin. There was both a moral code and best practices under the Jewish law. The covenant of grace was never meant to undermine the moral code. Holiness and love hold the moral code to a higher standard. In the New Testament, adultery began by merely lusting after a woman in your heart; in the Old Testament, the sin did not exist until it expressed itself through adultery. Again I turn to the wisdom of N. T. Wright to look at our day:

> Our modern world has turned sexual desire, preference and practice into a moral free-for-all, where the only rule is that people must be allowed to express whatever desires happen to arise, or be aroused, within them. For Paul, as for all Jewish and early Christian teachers of moral behaviour, that is like saying that you must allow the horse or donkey, unbroken and untamed, to rush and leap about in all directions, endangering rider and onlookers alike, and doing no useful

Running away isn't enough. We must run to something.

work. Sexuality is a good gift of the wise creator, but like all good gifts is given for a purpose; only in a world where the only purpose was self-gratification could anyone suppose that hard work was not going to be necessary to tame and train powerful desires such as the sexual one.[6]

Self-gratification should never be the goal for those who follow Christ. We cannot allow our appetites and sexual desires to be our master. Jesus was fully human and was tempted just as we are. This means he had the capacity to experience the same longings we each wrestle with. Yet he was sinless. Whatever that temptation might look like in your life, Jesus overcame it so that sin will not master you with its dominion. I am not saying that overcoming temptation will be easy. It will be hard, but freedom is worth the fight.

Holiness Means Telling the Truth

Just remember, when the unbelieving world hates you, they first hated me. If you were to give your allegiance to the world, they would love and welcome you as one of their own. But because you won't align yourself with the values of this world, they will hate you. I have chosen you and taken you out of the world to be mine. (John 15:18–19 TPT)

We are to stand in the middle of the chaos and declare truth. We will be hated if we choose to align ourselves with the values of the eternal. Being holy unto the Lord does not mean that people will always be happy with what we say. Jesus repeats his charge to remember yet again in the next verses:

So remember what I taught you, that a servant isn't superior to his master. And since they persecuted me, they will also persecute you. And if they obey my teachings, they will also obey yours. They will treat you this way because you are mine, and they don't know the One who sent me. (vv. 20–21 TPT)

We were promised persecution, not popularity. It is popular to go along with what the world says. It is popular to say that truth is subjective and the Bible is outdated. It is popular to say that Jesus understands your pain and unpopular to suggest that he might also empower you to walk with a limp rather than lean on your own understanding. It is not popular to say that the Word of God is our final authority in life. It is not popular to say that he is the God who changes not, even though our response to sin changes.

If I had not come and revealed myself to the unbelieving world, they would not feel the guilt of their sin, but now their sin is left uncovered. (John 15:22 TPT)

We do not remove guilt by normalizing and excusing sin; we must go to the root of the matter and remove the source of the guilt and shame—divided hearts.

As followers of Christ, we could never endorse cutting the hands off of thieves, killing adulterers, or capital punishment for those who commit incest or rape. Our goal is not to enforce the law; it is to point the way to Jesus. In Christ, all sins are forgiven and we remove ourselves from any position of judgment. Yet loving someone does not mean we *endorse* their transgressions (greed, idolatry, divination, or immorality). It means we acknowledge their human value and speak light into their future.

None of us are without sin, but that revelation doesn't mean wrong changes to right. Let's revisit the interaction in which Jesus asked the woman caught in adultery if there was anyone left to accuse her:

> She said, "No one, Lord." And Jesus said, "Neither do I condemn you; go, and from now on sin no more." (John 8:11)

Jesus did not stop with the mercy of forgiveness ("Neither do I condemn you"); he added in repentance and grace ("Go, and from now on sin no more"). He didn't endorse her lifestyle of adultery. He didn't say, "Don't worry about it, baby girl. All your future sins are forgiven." (Even though they were.) He didn't say, "I understand you have needs." He said, "Leave your life of shadow and walk in my light."

> Again Jesus spoke to them, saying, "I am the light of the world. Whoever follows me will not walk in darkness, but will have the light of life." (John 8:12)

Rather than leave the darkness for the light, we often change our point of view and call the darkness light.

Rather than leave the darkness for the light, we often change our point of view and call the darkness light. Let's walk in the empathy that empowers others to live lives of freedom. Let's invite others to leave behind the darkness of their pasts and to follow Jesus into his light. But this is one of those conversations best conducted privately, not hashed out on social media, which is why I am addressing it one-on-one with you.

> Do not give dogs what is holy, and do not throw your pearls before pigs, lest they trample them underfoot and turn to attack you. (Matt. 7:6)

I would not have had a frame of reference for the idea of holiness had I not become a student of the Scriptures. The Word of God outside the context of a loving Father sounds harsh. I don't want to tell you what to think. You already have far too many people doing that. I want you to think and hear for yourself. This is why I am asking you to study these Scripture passages and earnestly echo these words of Jesus's prayer for us:

> I have given them your word, and the world has hated them because they are not of the world, just as I am not of the world. I do not ask that you take them out of the world, but that you keep them from the evil one. They are not of the world, just as I am not of the world. Sanctify them in the truth; your word is truth. As you sent me into the world, so I have sent them into the world. And for their sake I consecrate myself, that they also may be sanctified in truth. (John 17:14–19)

Dear heavenly Father,
Sanctify me with your Word and make me holy in truth.
Empower me to leave behind any realm of shadow. I
want to live and love in the light of your leading. To be
holy in all I do so others know I belong to you.

11

I AM ADAMANT

A frame of adamant, a soul of fire,
No dangers fright him, and no labors tire.

Samuel Johnson

To tell how my journey toward adamant began, I will rewind time by more than a decade.

It started with a rough phone call with the freelance editor the publisher had hired to work with me on one of my books. The two of us had gone back and forth over both the book's content and tone. Sadly, I could no longer recognize my voice in the chapters she had edited. Due to a lack of confidence, I had allowed her to push me back all the way to the wall. I realized I could not push back any further and be obedient to what I had been told to write.

I knew this book was a message and a mandate that God had entrusted to me, and ultimately I would be the one to answer for how it was stewarded. For books are far more than collections of words on pages. They carry within them the cadence or tone and posture of the author. I believe how you read or hear a book is just as important as what you read. If the right thing is said in the wrong manner, an idea can be lost on the reader. For whatever reason, this editor had changed my tone to one of anger and my posture to that of an authoritarian. This was not the stance I wanted to adopt. When it comes to most topics, I am a fellow student of the Scriptures who wants to create communities of conversation. I prefer to speak as a sister, a mother, and now in this season a grandmother, even though my dearest hope is that you will allow me the greatest honor and for the duration of the pages call me friend.

My editor did not agree with this approach. She was a strong and talented woman with very definite opinions. I had hinted repeatedly, but I wasn't being heard. On this call, all hinting was over. John overheard the conversation as I put a fine point on my position and went over her edits word by word and sentence by sentence.

I hung up and breathed a heavy sigh. I was utterly exhausted after the interchange. I was working on the book in the dining room across from John's office.

"Rough phone call?" John suggested.

"Yes," I admitted.

"Is it going to work out?" he asked.

"I don't know," I answered truthfully.

John knew I had caved quite a bit in my former discussions with her.

"Well, this time you sounded . . . adamant." John volunteered the word as a vote of confidence.

I nodded.

Then suddenly it was as though his word choice ignited something dormant deep within me.

I stood up and affirmed his words. "I am adamant!"

And then to bring this declaration closer, I walked myself into John's office and repeated it. "I am adamant!"

John nodded his agreement. "Okay, then get back to work."

Life came into me.

I returned to my computer and reviewed the chapters I had already given up ground on and reworked them, and I recovered my voice in the book. I felt the fire of God's vision for the book quicken. As I worked, it was as though the words flew out of my fingertips.

Later that afternoon, my assistant came by with a package.

"You received an unusual gift," she said as she placed it on the table. She stood aside and watched for my reaction as I opened it.

It was a black rectangular box decorated with gold scroll-work details on the corners. As I opened it, an ornamental clear globe swung into view from the interior of the lid. The inside of the box was lined with gold velvet, and within its confines was a single piece of paper. Correction, paper is an understatement. It was a sheet of parchment with an opalescent finish. The lettering was the sort of font you'd use for a wedding invitation or a certificate of merit. It was dated December 12, 2005, and the word *diamond* appeared in the banner that hovered above the salutation "My Adamant, My Dearest Lisa, My Adamant."

I shivered. The fact that I had been asserting the same designation over myself a few hours earlier was not lost on me. Arrested, I sat down with the profound awareness that what I held was no ordinary letter. I caught my breath, released it, and read further.

In my hand was a poem that declared the strength of God's love over my life. Each sentence was woven with the words "I am." On this single page, the word *adamant* appeared five times. The words were intimate enough for me to feel seen by my Father. There was no name at the end of the page. I turned it over. Nothing.

"Who is it from?" I asked.

"We don't know," my assistant answered. "It came in a plainly wrapped package without a return address."

I was humbled that someone had listened to God and taken the time to write down these words for me, someone who didn't know I'd been questioning myself and struggling to write a book. God bless them. I took the gift as a sign and a confirmation that I was to stay the course with the direction of the manuscript, that I was to write without fear and tell my sisters that God has created you to be answers in a world fraught with problems.

> **God has created you to be answers in a world fraught with problems.**

I never learned who sent the package. Even so, I kept the box and its letter on top of the hutch over my desk. It was a memento of a turning point. The words marked the moment when I decided to be adamant, invincible, and immovable about what God spoke to me and how he spoke it. In the future, I would stay in my authority and not compromise.

Over the next year, I put letters in the box. (Remember those?) They were mostly testimonies from young girls and women who had been touched by the book. The box was not large, and it filled quickly. Then it remained unopened, collecting dust over the next decade.

Diamonds

Recently, I began to see diamonds everywhere. It seemed to be the common thread running through many of the conferences I spoke at over the course of a year. In all honesty, I'd forgotten the relationship between adamants and diamonds. Given the state of our world, I was of the opinion that centering events around the idea of diamonds was flashy and a bit superficial.

But there I was at yet another "diamond" conference. Slightly annoyed, I was in my hotel room between sessions and complaining within myself about the topic when in my spirit I heard, "You once rejoiced when I called you my diamond, my adamant."

Stunned, I remembered the poem. I sat down and opened the Bible software on my iPad. I began to search for references to diamonds or stones. When I came across the following reference in 1 Peter 2, I knew I was being led on a treasure hunt: "Welcome to the living Stone, the source of life" (v. 4 Message).

Within a week, I had found references in ancient texts that spoke of the word *adamant*. One manuscript of particular interest had been written in the 1600s. It referenced Ezekiel 3 and said how God had made the Son of Man's face like an adamant just as he had promised to do for Ezekiel.

I smiled at the reference to our Christ, who set his face as flint (adamant) to die that we might live.

The author went on to describe the adamant in many terms we have already become familiar with. The adamant is the hardest of stones: fire cannot burn it, heat cannot penetrate its core, a hammer cannot break its bond, the force of many waters cannot dissolve it. The adamant shrinks not, fears not, and changes not its hue. The adamant is constant. He closed out his thoughts on the matter with this conclusion: "A good conscience will make a Christian like an adamant, twill make him invincible and unchangeable."[1]

You are imprinted on his heart.

As we prepare to part ways, I feel it is only right that I share with you a portion of the poem I received, for I have no doubt that it contains promises that were meant to be shared. Each line is intimate and a unique call to each of us.

> My adamant,
> I smile when I AM in thought of you.
> You hear and know My voice well.
> You smile at My greatness.
> How I say, you are strong.
> Indeed, My adamant.
> May I sway your heart?
> I AM in great love with you.
> In great kindness I speak.
> As I AM, you are. I AM moved.
> My heart is imprinted by you.
> Honor Me with your beautiful smile and strong heart.
> My adamant.

Smile, lovely one. You are imprinted on his heart, and his words are spoken in kindness. Honor him, brave one, with the strength of your heart and the length of your days. Tell others of his adamant love. Honor his hand on your life with the royal authority of his Word and the anointing of his Holy Spirit.

Continuing in the vein of the poetic, allow me to paraphrase and personalize the lines from Samuel Johnson that I quoted at the beginning of the chapter. Dear one in Christ:

> You have a frame of adamant,
> And a soul of fire,
> No danger should frighten you,
> For adversity lifts you higher.

Our frame of adamant is transparent, radiant, magnetic, traced in light, yet as hard as diamond. We have been wrapped in the indestructible work of Christ. The Spirit of Christ dwells within us even as we dwell in Christ, our Adamant.

And let us now speak of this soul of fire:

> John answered them all, saying, "I baptize you with water, but he who is mightier than I is coming, the strap of whose sandals I am not worthy to untie. He will baptize you with the Holy Spirit and fire." (Luke 3:16)

We have been baptized in the Holy Spirit and with holy fire. John's baptism was an outward foreshadowing of what Jesus would work within us. When we were born again, our lifeless hearts were quickened by the fiery brilliance of his eternal love. Our God of holy fire consumes the chaff of shadow that would weaken the expression of his love to and through us. His fire encompasses us.

Zechariah 2:5 says, "'And I will be to her a wall of fire all around,' declares the LORD, 'and I will be the glory in her midst.'" The Message frames this fire as God's radiant presence within. I believe this verse speaks of both Jerusalem and Zion the church. As God is to Israel so he is to us. Likewise, we are surrounded by God's fiery, protective presence. David spoke of the angelic host in Psalm 104:4 by saying, "He makes his messengers winds, his ministers a flaming fire."

In Zechariah 13, fire is an instrument of purification:

> And I will put this third into the fire, and refine them as one refines silver, and test them as gold is tested. They will call upon my name, and I will answer them. I will say, "They are my people"; and they will say, "The LORD is my God." (v. 9)

In the fire, we call and he answers. It is there that he calls us his own and we realize that the Lord is our personal salvation.

In Genesis 15:17, our father of faith Abraham watched as the smoking pot and the flaming torch moved among the pieces of his offering. Our God is not asking us for divided offerings of calf, goat, ram, and birds. He requests that we surrender our hearts to the fire of his holiness.

> **Never ignore the gift on your life.**

Second Timothy 1:6 compares the gift God places in our lives to a flame that needs to be tended. Fan it, my friend. Sing. Dance. Read. Pray. Stay in fellowship. Witness. Get in a study group. Find a mentor. Rest, pause, and ponder. But never ignore the gift on your life. It is more precious than a diamond. Tend it more carefully than a garden. Make time for it and don't neglect it.

The next line of the personalized stanza is, "No danger should frighten you." We are protected without and purified within. Positioned in this manner, how could anything truly frighten us? Yes, we can expect to be startled and caught off guard, but if we live with this awareness, being frightened and afraid will be but passing phases, not a way of life.

And the last line: "For adversity lifts you higher." To illustrate this, I want to share a story told to me by a new friend. If you didn't already know this, you should: I love coffee . . . a lot. Actually, it is espresso that I am adamant about. I believe its dark lure is woven deep within the fiber of my Italian genes!

Do you know God can use something you love to get a message to you? And even if you are not a fan of java in any of its tantalizing forms, I believe this coffee shop tale is for you.

Recently, I stayed in downtown Amarillo, Texas. I was speaking at a women's conference and staying on for the weekend services. Whenever I check into a hotel, I inquire about the closest coffee shop. To my delight, I learned there was an exceptional one a mere block away . . . the award-winning Palace Coffee Company.

I had arrived too late on Friday night to partake, but after hearing the rave reviews, I set my alarm an hour earlier than needed for Saturday morning. As soon as my iPhone blared, I tumbled out of bed, brushed my teeth, slipped on the clothes I had laid out, donned my trusty aviators, and walked to this place of wonder.

To say I was excited would be an understatement. The place had a cool Texas hipster vibe, which I love, having birthed one son and inherited one daughter-in-law from the great Lone Star State. One glance at the drink menu and I was perfectly giddy.

When it was my turn, I leaned over the counter—I may have held her hands—and said to the cute barista, "Tell me all about your specialties."

"We have a microfoam cappuccino."

"Great." I had no idea what that was, so I probed further. "What else?"

"We have my favorite, which is a lavender latte," she offered.

"Okay." I nodded, affirming her preference. "Anything else?" I asked, trying to contain my rising excitement.

"We have a fig and honey latte as well."

"Perfect!" I answered, resisting a strong urge to hug her. "I want all three of them. Let's begin with the cappuccino and then move on to the lattes, but I will pay for all of them now." I gave my name, paid, and moved to the end of the counter.

What happened next caught me off guard. I don't know if he had been standing on my blind side or if I had been so caught up in beverage bliss that I had failed to notice him. I heard a male voice ask, "Are you from here?"

I turned to see the white-haired, white-bearded, handsome, and rather scholarly looking gentleman who had addressed me. "I'm not. I just heard about the coffee shop," I mumbled. I try to avoid conversation before caffeine.

"I just moved here," he volunteered.

I now had my microfoam in hand and was moving toward the cinnamon and raw sugar.

"Where are you from?" he asked.

"I'm from Colorado," I answered as I stirred my drink in anticipation.

"What brought you here?"

"I'm speaking at a women's conference where a few thousand women are gathered." Then I began to gush about how they had opened up the event to the community.

"Why aren't we covering this?"

Confused by his suggestion of coverage, I asked, "I don't know. Who are you?"

"I'm the new editor in chief of the local paper. Won't you join me? Please, sit down."

There was a moment of panic. Was I about to be interviewed before caffeine hit my bloodstream? I took a deep breath. There was kindness in his eyes, so I sat. I sipped while he fired questions my way.

"What type of conference is it? Where is this conference?" I had the distinct impression he was looking for something in my words.

I explained that the conference theme was based on one of my books (*Lioness Arising*) and I had been invited to minister. We asked the barista who knew all things for the address of the church.

"Did you read the article about the excavation of the catacombs?"

I assured him I had not.

My new friend explained that this excavation of the catacombs in Rome had revealed frescoes illustrating scenes from the early days of the church. I listened and sipped. Some of these frescoes clearly portrayed women, including Priscilla, ministering alongside the men.[2] I nodded, enjoying all that he shared. Then suddenly something shifted. He leaned back, looked at me as I hovered over my latte, and pointed. "You are one of those women!" he declared.

Somehow his words shot straight into my sleepy chest and reverberated to the core of my being. I was suddenly fully awake. I am not sure he was aware of the impact his words had on me. Before I realized what I was doing, we were exchanging contact information and he was forwarding me the article.

He apologized, "I can't be there tonight, but I am sending a reporter to cover your service, and I will be there in the morning."

I collected my next latte and sat back down. I listened as he shared his background and bits and pieces about his family. I shared a bit about my own, and before long it was time for me to head back to the hotel to get ready for the conference. As I walked back, I wondered, *What just happened?*

> My friend, God is in the process of rolling away the stones that have impeded your complete resurrection.

Later, I realized that what he spoke to me was not just for me. God wanted it declared to a generation of women who had been buried in a maze of life's subterranean chambers.

My friend, God is in the process of rolling away the stones that have impeded your complete resurrection. He is clearing away the rubble and debris. And all those broken pieces that you thought were wasted or lost? Lift your head, lovely one, and look; he has used them to make a mosaic out of your life. You have been so busy looking down at the mess that you have missed the banner he is weaving over your life. "You are one of those women!"

> To whom then will you compare me, that I should be like him? says the Holy One. Lift up your eyes on high and see: who created these? He who brings out their host by number, calling them all by name; *by the greatness of his might and because he is strong in power, not one is missing.* (Isa. 40:25–26)

Nothing lost, nothing wasted, not one piece missing. Buried under so many layers of dust, dirt, and broken stone is yet another page of our story.

When I read the article for myself, I saw a mosaic of a robed woman with her arms open in benediction and welcome.

Forget for a moment the gravediggers. Push away all thoughts of those who heaped dirt, debris, and rubble in an attempt to bury you alive. Turn from them and ask, "What is it the enemy wanted buried in your life?"

The seed might be in the form of a hope, a dream, a prayer, a promise, or even tears. The seed may be outside your sight, but don't imagine for a minute that it is off God's mind.

What we sow does not come to life unless it dies (1 Cor. 15:36). Hardship serves as our preparation.

In so many ways and in so many places, the story of God's daughters has been buried just as in so many ways the story of Christ's beautiful bride has been muddied. Even so remember, lovely one, all that was hidden will one day be revealed. Just as with the excavation of the catacombs, the story of the bride is breaking out again into the light.

We are those women.

We are his bride.

His diamonds.

His priceless treasure.

He is our Adamant, our Anchor, our Truth.

He is the Rock that follows us through each of our wildernesses.

Lift your life and honor the Stone from which you were hewn. Live in wonder of the immovable, invincible, impervious, adamant Cornerstone who longs to astound you with his loving faithfulness. Be true to him in this universe of opinions, for you are marked for the eternal realm.

APPENDIX 1

ADDITIONAL SCRIPTURE PASSAGES FOR CHAPTER 6

You shall not make for yourself a carved image, or any likeness of anything that is in heaven above, or that is in the earth beneath, or that is in the water under the earth. You shall not bow down to them or serve them, for I the LORD your God am a jealous God, visiting the iniquity of the fathers on the children to the third and the fourth generation of those who hate me, but showing steadfast love to thousands of those who love me and keep my commandments. (Exod. 20:4–6)

If you spurn my statutes, and if your soul abhors my rules, so that you will not do all my commandments, but break my covenant, then I will do this to you: I will visit you with panic, with wasting disease and fever that consume the eyes and make the heart ache. And you shall sow your seed in vain, for your enemies shall eat it. I will set my face against you, and you shall be struck down before your enemies. Those who hate you shall rule over you, and you shall flee when none pursues you. (Lev. 26:15–17)

But Jehu the son of Hanani the seer went out to meet him and said to King Jehoshaphat, "Should you help the wicked and love those who hate the LORD? Because of this, wrath has gone out against you from the LORD. Nevertheless, some good is found in you, for you destroyed the Asheroth out of the land, and have set your heart to seek God." (2 Chron. 19:2–3)

> For you are not a God who delights in wickedness;
>   evil may not dwell with you.
> The boastful shall not stand before your eyes;
>   you hate all evildoers.
> You destroy those who speak lies;
>   the LORD abhors the bloodthirsty and deceitful
>   man.
> But I, through the abundance of your steadfast love,
>   will enter your house.
> I will bow down toward your holy temple
>   in the fear of you. (Ps. 5:4–7)

> His glory is great through your salvation;
>   splendor and majesty you bestow on him.
> For you make him most blessed forever;
>   you make him glad with the joy of your presence.
> For the king trusts in the LORD,
>   and through the steadfast love of the Most High
>   he shall not be moved.
> Your hand will find out all your enemies;
>   your right hand will find out those who hate you.
>   (Ps. 21:5–8)

O you who love the LORD, hate evil!
    He preserves the lives of his saints;
    he delivers them from the hand of the wicked.
Light is sown for the righteous,
    and joy for the upright in heart.
Rejoice in the LORD, O you righteous,
    and give thanks to his holy name! (Ps. 97:10–12)

I hold back my feet from every evil way,
    in order to keep your word.
I do not turn aside from your rules,
    for you have taught me.
How sweet are your words to my taste,
    sweeter than honey to my mouth!
Through your precepts I get understanding;
    therefore I hate every false way. (Ps. 119:101–4)

Therefore I love your commandments
    above gold, above fine gold.
Therefore I consider all your precepts to be right;
    I hate every false way. (Ps. 119:127–28)

I rejoice at your word
    like one who finds great spoil.
I hate and abhor falsehood,
    but I love your law. (Ps. 119:162–63)

They speak against you with malicious intent;
    your enemies take your name in vain.
Do I not hate those who hate you, O LORD?
    And do I not loathe those who rise up against
      you?
I hate them with complete hatred;
    I count them my enemies. (Ps. 139:20–22)

> Righteousness guards him whose way is blameless,
> but sin overthrows the wicked. (Prov. 13:6)

Whoever is not with me is against me, and whoever does not gather with me scatters. (Matt. 12:30)

But I say to you who hear, Love your enemies, do good to those who hate you. (Luke 6:27)

Now great crowds accompanied him, and he turned and said to them, "If anyone comes to me and does not hate his own father and mother and wife and children and brothers and sisters, yes, and even his own life, he cannot be my disciple. (Luke 14:25–26)

So therefore, any one of you who does not renounce all that he has cannot be my disciple. (Luke 14:33)

The Pharisees, who were lovers of money, heard all these things, and they ridiculed him. And he said to them, "You are those who justify yourselves before men, but God knows your hearts. For what is exalted among men is an abomination in the sight of God. The Law and the Prophets were until John; since then the good news of the kingdom of God is preached, and everyone forces his way into it. But it is easier for heaven and earth to pass away than for one dot of the Law to become void." (Luke 16:14–17)

Jesus said to them, "My time has not yet come, but your time is always here. The world cannot hate you, but it hates me because I testify about it that its works are evil." (John 7:6–7)

APPENDIX 2

LESSONS FROM PROVERBS AND ECCLESIASTES

Be Teachable and Don't Babble

> The wise of heart will receive commandments,
> but a babbling fool will come to ruin. (Prov. 10:8)

Words Can Refresh and Restore Life or Hide What Takes It

> The mouth of the righteous is a fountain of life,
> but the mouth of the wicked conceals violence.
> (Prov. 10:11)

> Open your mouth for the mute,
> for the rights of all who are destitute. (Prov. 31:8)

Open your mouth, judge righteously,
> defend the rights of the poor and needy.
> (Prov. 31:9)

She opens her mouth with wisdom,
> and the teaching of kindness is on her tongue.
> (Prov. 31:26)

Hatred Stirs the Pot, and Love Puts a Lid on It

Hatred stirs up strife,
> but love covers all offenses. (Prov. 10:12)

Scoffers set a city aflame,
> but the wise turn away wrath. (Prov. 29:8)

There are those whose teeth are swords,
> whose fangs are knives,
to devour the poor from off the earth,
> the needy from among mankind. (Prov. 30:14)

The Mouth of a Fool Gets Him in Trouble

On the lips of him who has understanding, wisdom
> is found,
> but a rod is for the back of him who lacks sense.
> (Prov. 10:13)

The wise lay up knowledge,
> but the mouth of a fool brings ruin near.
> (Prov. 10:14)

The one who conceals hatred has lying lips,
   and whoever utters slander is a fool. (Prov. 10:18)

The words of a wise man's mouth win him favor,
   but the lips of a fool consume him. (Eccles. 10:12)

The beginning of the words of his mouth is
      foolishness,
   and the end of his talk is evil madness.
      (Eccles. 10:13)

A fool multiplies words,
   though no man knows what is to be,
   and who can tell him what will be after him?
      (Eccles. 10:14)

Don't Let It Get to You

The vexation of a fool is known at once,
   but the prudent ignores an insult. (Prov. 12:16)

Whoever speaks the truth gives honest evidence,
   but a false witness utters deceit. (Prov. 12:17)

There is one whose rash words are like sword
      thrusts,
   but the tongue of the wise brings healing.
      (Prov. 12:18)

The Truth Will Always Outlive a Lie

> There is one whose rash words are like sword
> thrusts,
> but the tongue of the wise brings healing.
> (Prov. 12:18)

> Truthful lips endure forever,
> but a lying tongue is but for a moment.
> (Prov. 12:19)

> A wicked messenger falls into trouble,
> but a faithful envoy brings healing. (Prov. 13:17)

> The simple believes everything,
> but the prudent gives thought to his steps.
> One who is wise is cautious and turns away from
> evil,
> but a fool is reckless and careless.
> A man of quick temper acts foolishly,
> and a man of evil devices is hated.
> (Prov. 14:15–17)

> A soft answer turns away wrath,
> but a harsh word stirs up anger. (Prov. 15:1)

> The tongue of the wise commends knowledge,
> but the mouths of fools pour out folly. (Prov. 15:2)

> A gentle tongue is a tree of life,
> but perverseness in it breaks the spirit. (Prov. 15:4)

> Fine speech is not becoming to a fool;
> still less is false speech to a prince. (Prov. 17:7)

Whoever covers an offense seeks love,
but he who repeats a matter separates close
friends. (Prov. 17:9)

Even a fool who keeps silent is considered wise;
when he closes his lips, he is deemed intelligent.
(Prov. 17:28)

A fool takes no pleasure in understanding,
but only in expressing his opinion. (Prov. 18:2)

The words of a man's mouth are deep waters;
the fountain of wisdom is a bubbling brook.
(Prov. 18:4)

A fool's lips walk into a fight,
and his mouth invites a beating. (Prov. 18:6)

A fool's mouth is his ruin,
and his lips are a snare to his soul. (Prov. 18:7)

The words of a whisperer are like delicious morsels;
they go down into the inner parts of the body.
(Prov. 18:8)

If one gives an answer before he hears,
it is his folly and shame. (Prov. 18:13)

It is an honor for a man to keep aloof from strife,
but every fool will be quarreling. (Prov. 20:3)

Whoever goes about slandering reveals secrets;
therefore do not associate with a simple babbler.
(Prov. 20:19)

If one curses his father or his mother,
    his lamp will be put out in utter darkness.
      (Prov. 20:20)

Do not say, "I will repay evil";
    wait for the LORD, and he will deliver you.
      (Prov. 20:22)

Whoever keeps his mouth and his tongue
    keeps himself out of trouble. (Prov. 21:23)

Drive out a scoffer, and strife will go out,
    and quarreling and abuse will cease. (Prov. 22:10)

Do not say, "I will do to him as he has done to me;
    I will pay the man back for what he has done."
      (Prov. 24:29)

Know Your Audience

Do not speak in the hearing of a fool,
    for he will despise the good sense of your words.
      (Prov. 23:9)

Fools Aren't Worthy of Your Time and Attention

Answer not a fool according to his folly,
    lest you be like him yourself.
Answer a fool according to his folly,
    lest he be wise in his own eyes. (Prov. 26:4–5)

If a wise man has an argument with a fool,
  the fool only rages and laughs, and there is no
  quiet. (Prov. 29:9)

If a Situation Doesn't Involve You, Don't Get Involved

Whoever meddles in a quarrel not his own
  is like one who takes a passing dog by the ears.
  (Prov. 26:17)

Gossip Will Burn You and Give You Indigestion

For lack of wood the fire goes out,
  and where there is no whisperer, quarreling ceases.
As charcoal to hot embers and wood to fire,
  so is a quarrelsome man for kindling strife.
The words of a whisperer are like delicious morsels;
  they go down into the inner parts of the body.
Like the glaze covering an earthen vessel
  are fervent lips with an evil heart. (Prov. 26:20–23)

A lying tongue hates its victims,
  and a flattering mouth works ruin. (Prov. 26:28)

Don't Brag

Let another praise you, and not your own mouth;
  a stranger, and not your own lips. (Prov. 27:2)

The crucible is for silver, and the furnace is for gold,
  and a man is tested by his praise. (Prov. 27:21)

A fool gives full vent to his spirit,
    but a wise man quietly holds it back. (Prov. 29:11)

If you have been foolish, exalting yourself,
    or if you have been devising evil,
    put your hand on your mouth. (Prov. 30:32)

NOTES

Chapter 1 The Adamant

1. N. T. Wright, *Matthew for Everyone, Part 2: Chapters 16–28* (London: Society for Promoting Christian Knowledge, 2004), 80.

2. Anthony C. Thiselton, *The First Epistle to the Corinthians: A Commentary on the Greek Text*, New International Greek Testament Commentary (Grand Rapids: Eerdmans, 2000).

3. Matthew G. Easton, *Easton's Bible Dictionary*, 1893.

4. John Muir, *My First Summer in the Sierra* (New York: Houghton Mifflin, 1911), 20.

Chapter 2 Adamantly Intimate

1. Babylonian Talmud, Chagigah 15.1: And the Spirit of God hovered [**merachefet**: from the Hebrew root "**rachaf**" (in the **feminine form**)] over the face of the water—like a dove which hovers over **her young** without touching.

2. C. S. Lewis, *Prince Caspian* (New York: HarperCollins 1951), 233.

Chapter 4 Adamant in Love

1. 2 Corinthians, The Passion Translation (Racine, WI: BroadStreet Publishing, 2017).

2. Composition/Song Title: Reckless Love. Written by Cory Asbury, Caleb Culver, and Ran Jackson © 2017 Bethel Music Publishing (ASCAP) / Watershed Publishing Group (ASCAP) (adm. by Watershed Music Group) / Richmond Park Publishing (BMI). All Rights Reserved. Used by Permission.

Chapter 5 Adamant That We Love

1. C. S. Lewis, *Mere Christianity* (New York: HarperCollins, 1952), 132.

Chapter 6 Adamant in Hate

1. Lewis, *Mere Christianity*, 112.

2. Gene Veith, "Sex as Sacrament, Abortion as Religious Ritual," *Cranach: The Blog of Veith*, June 24, 2016, http://www.patheos.com/blogs/geneveith/2016/06/sex-as-sacrament-abortion-as-religious-ritual/.

3. Charles H. Spurgeon, *The Complete Works of C. H. Spurgeon, Vol. 44: Sermons 2459–2602* (Delmarva Publications, 2013).

4. "Study Finds That 1 Out of 3 Women Watch Porn at Least Once a Week," *New York Times*, October 22, 2015.

5. Alexis Kleinman, "Porn Sites Get More Visitors Each Month Than Netflix, Amazon, and Twitter Combined," *Huffington Post*, May 3, 2013, http://www.huffingtonpost.com/2013/05/03/internet-porn-stats_n_3187682.html.

6. "How Many People Are Watching Porn Right Now? (Hint: It's A Lot.)," Fight the New Drug, September 11, 2017, http://fightthenewdrug.org/by-the-numbers-see-how-many-people-are-watching-porn-today/.

7. Charles H. Spurgeon, *The Complete Works of C. H. Spurgeon, Vol. 60: Sermons 3387–3349* (Delmarva Publications, 2013).

8. https://www.leadershipresources.org/blog/the-best-charles-spurgeon-quotes/.

9. "Charles H. Spurgeon on Discernment" *Apologetics* 315, www.apologetics 315.com, Feb 3, 2013.

Chapter 8 Adamant in Word

1. Shaena Montanari, "Plastic Garbage Patch Bigger than Mexico Found in Pacific," *National Geographic*, July 25, 2017, http://news.nationalgeographic.com/2017/07/ocean-plastic-patch-south-pacific-spd.

2. Leonardo da Vinci, *Notebooks* (Oxford: Oxford University Press, 1952), 23.

Chapter 9 Adamant Transformation

1. Preston Sprinkle, *People to Be Loved* (Grand Rapids: Zondervan, 2015), 88.

2. C. S. Lewis, *Surprised by Joy: The Shape of My Early Life* (Orlando: Harcourt Brace & Company, 1955), 221.

3. Tom Carter, compiler. *Spurgeon at His Best: Over 2200 Striking Quotations from the World's Most Exhaustive and Widely Read Sermon Series* (Grand Rapids: Baker Books, 1988), 160.

Chapter 10 Adamant in Holiness

1. Sinclair Ferguson, *A Heart for God* (Carlisle, PA: Banner of Truth, 1987), 82.

2. N. T. Wright, *Paul for Everyone: Galatians and Thessalonians* (London: Society for Promoting Christian Knowledge, 2004), 117–18.

3. Carter, compiler. *Spurgeon at His Best*, 100.

4. Kevin M. Watson, "Forgiveness and (Not Or) Holiness," *Vital Piety* (blog), August 26, 2013, https://vitalpiety.com/2013/08/26/forgiveness-and-not-or-holiness/.

5. N. T. Wright, *Paul for Everyone: The Prison Letters: Ephesians, Philippians, Colossians, and Philemon* (London: Society for Promoting Christian Knowledge, 2004), 53.

6. Wright, *Paul for Everyone: Galatians and Thessalonians*, 118–19.

Chapter 11 I Am Adamant

1. Charles H. Spurgeon, *Treasury of David Vol. 3* (New York: Funk & Wagnalls, 1886), 278.

2. Ellie Zolfagharifard, "Vatican Unveils Frescoes Hinting That Women Held Power in the Early Church," *Daily Mail*, November 20, 2013.

Lisa Bevere has spent nearly three decades empowering women of all ages to find their identity and purpose. She is a *New York Times* bestselling author and internationally known speaker. Her previous books, which include *Fight Like a Girl*, *Lioness Arising*, *Girls with Swords*, and *Without Rival*, are in the hands of millions worldwide. Lisa and her husband, John, are the founders of Messenger International, an organization committed to developing uncompromising followers of Christ who transform their world.

ADAMANT

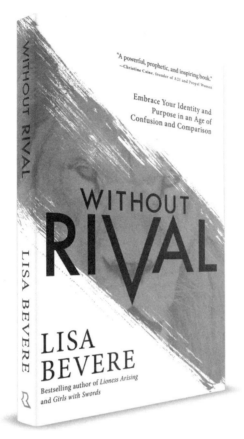

BOOKS BY LISA

Without Rival*
Be Angry but Don't Blow It!
Fight Like a Girl*
Girls with Swords*
It's Not How You Look, It's What You See
Lioness Arising*

Kissed the Girls and Made Them Cry*
Nurture*
Out of Control and Loving It!
The True Measure of a Woman
You Are Not What You Weigh

*Available in study format

Messenger International exists to develop
uncompromising followers of Christ who
transform our world.

Call: **1-800-648-1477**

Visit us online at: **MessengerInternational.org**

Connect with Lisa Bevere

LisaBevere.com